PATTERNS FOR POWER

A Bible Commentary for Laymen/Parables of Luke
BY D. STUART BRISCOE

 A Division of GL Publications
Ventura, CA 93006

Other good reading:

Bound for Joy, the study of Philippians,
   by D. Stuart Briscoe

Let's Get Moving, the study of Ephesians,
   by D. Stuart Briscoe

Always a Winner, the study of 1 Samuel,
   by Cyril Barber and John Carter

How It All Began, the study of Genesis 1–11,
   by Ronald Youngblood

The foreign language publishing of all Regal books is under the direction of GLINT. GLINT provides financial and technical help for the adaptation, translation and publishing of books in more than 85 languages for millions of people worldwide.

For more information write: GLINT, Ventura, California 93006.

Scripture quotations in this publication are from the *New International Version,* Holy Bible. Copyright © 1978 by New York International Bible Society.

Second Printing, 1979

Published by Regal Books
A Division of GL Publications
Ventura, California 93006
Printed in U.S.A.

Library of Congress Catalog Card No. 78-68850
ISBN 0-8307-0701-8

Contents

A Teacher's Manual and Student Discovery Guide for Bible Study groups using *Patterns for Power* are available from your church supplier.

Introduction

Most people agree that Jesus was a superb communicator. The crowds that surrounded Him wherever He went did so not only because of His penchant for miracles but also because of His skill with words. He always had something pungent and relevant to say and the crowds loved it. This did not mean that they necessarily understood what He was saying or obeyed what He was commanding, but they attended the talks nevertheless. This lack of comprehension and failure to follow through was particularly frustrating to the Master. The readiness of the people to be entertained contrasted starkly with their lack of readiness to respond to the moral, ethical and spiritual ramifications of what He was saying. This led Him to adopt a special style of speaking. He told the people parables.

His use of parables was a calculated effort on His part to get His listeners to think about what He was saying rather than spend their time enjoying the way He said it. His great desire was that they should progress from an immature listening to His words, to a mature hearing and application of the content of His message. If they would be prepared to concentrate on the parable and respond to the principles enunciated in the parable they would be blessed, but if they persisted in their shallow uninvolved approach they would miss the blessing as well as the point.

But what exactly is a parable? When I was a small boy in England my teacher taught me to say, "A parable is an earthly story with a heavenly meaning." When one of my fellow students was asked to give the definition we had learned he almost got it right: "A parable is a earthy story with a heavy meaning."

The word comes from two Greek words *para*, meaning "alongside," and *bole*, which is the verb "to throw." So *parable* means literally, "to throw alongside" or "to compare." A parable is a story designed to compare that which is patently obvious to that which may not be obvious at all. It has a special significance in Christ's ministry because He used parables to illustrate the invisible things of the spirit from the visible and readily understandable things of everyday life. Because the stories were so earthly and easy the casual listeners continued to be entertained, but because they were so full of deep spiritual significance those who were prepared to think them through and follow them through derived untold spiritual blessings from the Master's teachings.

The study of the parables has fascinated Christians throughout the history of the Christian church no less than it fascinated the disciples who heard the stories when they were first told. Modern believers should take heart that even the early disciples sometimes had problems getting the point of the Master's stories, but we, like they, can always discover that He is always ready to assist us in our search for truth.

In medieval times biblical scholars used a four-fold method of biblical interpretation which was known as the *quadriga*. They believed that every text should yield four meanings: literal, moral, allegorical, and anagogical. When they approached the parables they had a field day as you may well imagine. Every detail of the stories was squeezed to yield its last drop of moral, allegorical or anagogical truth. The parable of the Good Samaritan was a rich vein for them. The story of the Prodigal Son yielded untold treasures as donkeys and swine, pennies and rings developed significance of the broadest possible dimensions. But by the time of the Reformation, things had changed and this style of interpretation was rejected by Luther and others, even though they were not too reluctant to indulge their own flights of fancy once in a while.

The approach in this book has been simply to look at the story in its context, to examine the circumstances in which it was told, to look at the questions that stimulated its telling or the actions that prompted its reaction. Each story holds one basic secret as it speaks to one fundamental issue, and each of these issues was so vital that the Master Himself felt He must address it in such a way that serious-minded listeners would get the message. His issues were power packed and as His words are studied today, contemporary readers will find them to be nothing less than "patterns for power" in our modern world.

Stuart Briscoe

1 Forgiveness— Liable to Be Loved

Luke 7:36-50—The Two Debtors

Now one of the Pharisees invited Jesus to have dinner with him, so he went to the Pharisee's house and reclined at the table. When a woman who lived a sinful life in that town learned that Jesus was eating at the Pharisee's house, she brought an alabaster jar of perfume, and as she stood behind him at his feet weeping, she began to wet his feet with her tears. Then she wiped them with her hair, kissed them and poured perfume on them.

When the Pharisee who had invited him saw this, he said to himself, "If this man were a prophet, he would know who is touching him and what kind of woman she is—that she is a sinner."

Jesus answered him, "Simon, I have something to tell you."

"Tell me, teacher," he said.

"Two men owed money to a certain moneylender. One owed him five hundred denarii, and the other fifty. Neither of them had the money to pay him back, so he canceled the debts of both. Now which of them will love him more?"

Simon replied, "I suppose the one who had the bigger debt canceled."

"You have judged correctly," Jesus said.

Then he turned toward the woman and said to Simon, "Do you see this woman? I came into your house. You did not give me any water for my feet, but she wet my feet with her tears and wiped them with her hair. You did not give me a kiss, but this woman, from the time I entered, has not stopped kissing my feet. You did not put oil on my head, but she has poured perfume on my feet. Therefore, I tell you, her many sins have been forgiven—for she loved much. But he who has been forgiven little loves little."

Then Jesus said to her, "Your sins are forgiven."

The other guests began to say among themselves, "Who is this who even forgives sins?"

Jesus said to the woman, "Your faith has saved you; go in peace."

Simon the Pharisee was having a hard time. The young preacher from Galilee was the cause of his problem. This preacher was moving around the area speaking His mind about many things dear to a Pharisee's heart and most of the things He was saying were intensely embarrassing. He had a frustrating and infuriating ability to expose hypocrisy and to shoot dead orthodoxy full of holes. As if that wasn't bad enough His life-style was enough to give any self-respecting Pharisee a heart attack. He appeared to have no idea of keeping His distance from undesirables. In fact, He almost seemed to take delight in seeking out that kind of person.

While the Pharisees hated what the preacher was saying and doing the common people loved every minute of it. So Simon came to the conclusion that something ought to be done to discredit Him. But that was easier said than done. Then Simon had a great idea. He would invite Jesus to dinner and see if he couldn't find something about Jesus that would give him some leverage. Of course, there was always the possibility that Jesus might turn him down but if He did Simon would be able to make a lot of mileage out of that by pointing out to all who would listen that Jesus would eat with the "riff-raff" but avoided the "society people." Simon decided it was worth a try. To Simon's delight, Jesus accepted.

The Unwelcome Welcome

In those days it was customary for a host to greet his guest with a kiss. Then a servant would remove the visitor's sandals and wash the dust from his travel-stained feet. Also, olive oil was provided for the new arrival to "freshen up" if he so desired. But when Jesus arrived at Simon's front door He received a most unwelcome welcome. No kiss, no water, no olive oil. Nothing but the cold shoulder. It was just as if you "welcomed" someone to your house by ignoring him, refusing to shake hands with him, left him standing in the hallway in his wet clothes and didn't bother to show him where he could hang his coat or wash his hands.

It is hard to believe that Simon was always as uncouth as this, and it would appear that his behavior was either carefully planned or an indication of his total disdain of Jesus. Whatever the cause there is no doubt about the effect. Jesus followed His inhospitable host into the dining room and reclined at table possibly feeling more than a little uncomfortable.

In circumstances like that even a hot meal would feel chilled!

Strange as it appears to our Western minds it was perfectly permissible for the village people to sit around the walls of the dining room during the meal so that they at least got in on the conversation even if they didn't make the guest list. With such a personality as the miracle-working preacher from Galilee as the guest there would, in all probability, be quite a crowd at Simon's place that evening. It should be pointed out, however, that not everyone was welcome to sit around in Simon's house. Because of his strong stance on moral, religious, and ethical matters the Pharisee would not be prepared to welcome anyone whose life-style did not equate to his own. Imagine his chagrin when just such a person walked in during the meal.

The Immoral Intruder

The woman was well-known for her immoral life; in fact, Simon thought of her as nothing short of a prostitute. To his intense dismay and annoyance she stood at Jesus' feet as He reclined at the table. Then she loosened her hair (an unthinkable action in public) and with tears streaming down her face onto His feet she alternately wiped them with her hair and kissed them. Then, breaking the long neck of the alabaster vase she was carrying, she poured the perfumed contents over Jesus' feet. Crying, kissing, pouring, wiping, the woman lavished her attention on Jesus who neither spoke nor moved.

But while Jesus remained calm Simon was in a turmoil. His immediate reaction to such an intrusion would have been to eject the woman from his home, but suddenly he saw how the woman might unwittingly have given him the chance he was seeking. Watching her every action and Jesus' every reaction he thought to himself, "This man claims to be a prophet but if He were a prophet He would certainly know about this woman and He would have nothing to do with her. So either He doesn't know what she is, in which case He's no prophet, or He does know and doesn't seem to mind, in which case He's a disgrace to the prophetic profession. So, either way, I can discredit Him." Little did Simon know that his guest was reading his thoughts like an open book.

The Two Debtors

With the woman continuing her activities and the people's attention riveted on her every move, Jesus spoke.

"Simon there were two men who fell on hard times and had to borrow money from the moneylender. One of them got into big trouble and ran up a debt amounting to about twenty-month's salary, the other borrowed about two-month's worth. Unfortunately, neither was able to repay the debt, but the moneylender was remarkably generous in that he cancelled both the large and small indebtedness. Now tell me, Simon, who would be most grateful, the one forgiven much or the one forgiven little?" Simon, who was in no mood for stories, answered rather patronizingly, "I suppose the one who was forgiven most."

"You're quite right, Simon, now let me tell you something. When I came into your house you neither welcomed me nor extended to me the common courtesies. In fact, you were downright rude. But this woman has been exactly the opposite. She has lavished love on me. You wouldn't kiss my cheek, she kissed my feet. You wouldn't even let your servant wash my feet, she washed them with tears and wiped them with her hair. You gave no anointing oil even though it is so cheap—you have more than you know what to do with—she poured priceless oil over me."

Simon was speechless. The crowd sat silently by. The woman wept quietly listening to every word from the Master. "Simon," Jesus went on, "this woman has behaved in this fashion because she knows what it is to be forgiven. She has been forgiven much so she loves much, just like the man who was forgiven the enormous debt. But you, by your lack of love, exhibit an appalling ignorance of what it means to be forgiven."

Turning to the woman He added, "Your sins are forgiven. Your faith has saved you. Go in peace."

With those words the silence was broken. Everybody started talking at once. "Who is this man who says He can forgive sins?" How long they stayed in Simon's house talking excitedly about the sensational events at the dinner party we are not told. What happened to Simon is a mystery too. But we do know that the woman went on her way rejoicing in her experience of forgiveness and expressing her love for her forgiver and we know that Jesus left us with a striking parable that we need to study carefully.

We Are All in God's Debt

When Jesus told Simon about the two creditors it was obvious to the point of embarrassment that He was referring to His supercilious host and the woman who had gate-crashed the party. But what He was saying also had relevance to all the people sitting around the room, because they were all confronted with the moral excellence of Jesus as He spoke to them. There was always something unsettling and unnerving about the presence of Jesus. He had the ability to bring a sense of conviction to the most self-righteous person. As we read the story of how He exposed Simon, I have little doubt that we too experience a similar sense of unworthiness. Like Simon we can spend our days living by our own standards, supported by those who have the same convictions, and assuming that we are living perfectly satisfactory lives. But confrontation with Jesus explodes that kind of thinking because it brings us face to face with God's requirements. Both in His teaching and in His life-style Jesus showed what God regards as normal behavior and, therefore, any honest confrontation with Him leads to a sense of moral failure in the eyes of God.

Jesus took the resources that the Father gave to Him and used them to the glory of the Father and the fulfillment of the Father's plan. We have received the resources of life and health, gifts and opportunities, time and energy, but instead of doing what Jesus did with His God-given resources, we have used them for ourselves and been anxious for our own glory and committed to our own plans. To this extent we are in debt to God for misuse and abuse of His provision.

We Are All Responsible for Our Debt

Ever since Adam got caught in the garden and promptly tried to blame both God and his own wife for his action, man has endeavored to evade his responsibilities. He has been greatly assisted by deterministic philosophies which have assured him that he is what he is because of his past over which he had no control, and he does what he does because of factors that have made him what he is.

It would be foolish to deny that both environment and heritage play an important part in our character development. As many a man in a prison cell will

13

testify, he certainly could not help being born in a poor family in an area of the city with a high crime rate. The school which he attended was not his choice and the kids who led him astray were the only kids around so his rapid slide into crime was predictable. But all kids brought up in a deprived environment do not take the route of crime, and many kids raised in superb circumstances end up in jail. So while we may say the kid with a bad background may *predictably* go wrong, we cannot say he will *inevitably* go wrong; because he is not a robot programmed to go only one way, he is a human who has the moral capability to choose to do right and refuse to do wrong.

To say that we are not responsible for our actions may get us off the hook for a while, but it leaves us in a fool's paradise where we play irresponsibly while building up an ever-increasing debt for which we are ultimately responsible. In the same way the two debtors in the parable discovered they were responsible for their debts regardless of the circumstances that led them to the point of penury, we too must stop making excuses and must terminate all evasive action and face up to our moral bankruptcy before God.

We Have Incurred Differing Degrees of Debt

Many people are offended by being accused of wrongdoing because they feel, quite rightly, that they have lived respectable lives and should not be placed in the same category as reprobates. Jesus was careful to show that He certainly didn't think that a Pharisee was as morally reprehensible as a prostitute, but He refused to allow the Pharisee to think that he was therefore perfect. The debtors were in debt for varying amounts, but they had two things in common nevertheless: they were both debtors and neither of them could pay. There is a dangerous tendency among "respectable" people to look with horror at those whom they regard as morally inferior, and at the same time to overlook or ignore Paul's statement, "There is no difference, for all have sinned and fall short of the glory of God" (Rom. 3:22,23).

We Are Incapable of Repaying Our Debts

To be aware of moral failure and ultimate responsibility can lead many people to seek ways of rectifying the situation. Because we have been trained to confront our problems and to work towards solutions, it is only natural for earnest people to look for ways to repay their debts to God. Many feel that a life of service to their fellowman or even a commitment to the ministry or the mission field will earn enough spiritual currency to pay off their spiritual debts. Others, much less earnest, somewhat casually embrace a Christian affiliation and embark on a nondescript Christian experience assuming that in some way their "good living" will cancel out their former misdemeanors.

In biblical times this kind of thinking was called "works"—that is, the people seeking to get right with God thought that they could merit divine favor if they worked hard enough at whatever they thought their God would require. But many passages of Scripture are devoted to showing that "no one," on this basis, will be declared righteous (Rom. 3:20). Like the men in the parable we don't have "the money to pay [God] back."

Hard as it may be we must all come to the position expressed by Augustus M. Toplady in his well known hymn, "Rock of Ages":

Not the labors of my hands,
Can fulfill Thy law's demands:

Could my zeal no respite know,
Could my tears forever flow,
All for sin could not atone;
Thou must save, and Thou alone.

There comes a time in every bankrupt person's life when he faces up to the fact that he cannot get himself out of his hole. At that point he may decide to use any avenue of escape that he may deem suitable or he may go to his creditors, lay his cards on the table and ask for mercy.

The force of the parable is in the statement that the creditor "canceled the debts of both." In normal business life this kind of reaction is rare but in the economy of God we are told that "he will freely pardon" (Isa. 55:7). This is surely one of the greatest pieces of information ever made known to man. Yet it is a sad reflection on contemporary society that for many people it is either a fact of which they are ignorant or a truth which they consider irrelevant.

The Forgiver Must Assume the Debt

Recently, in conversation with a young man who was troubled about his moral bankruptcy and responsibility toward God, I tried to explain the fact that God is ready to "freely pardon." He shook his head and said, "That's too easy. What I've done can't be easily forgotten."

I find many people stumble over the same thing. But as I pointed out to the young man we must not assume that because pardon is free it is cheap, any more than we can assume that a creditor can cancel a debt without having to pay it himself.

We don't need to be experts in bookkeeping to realize that if you owe me $1,000 and fail to repay me that means I have lost $1,000. I can't just say, "Forget it. It doesn't matter." The simple fact of the matter

16

is that I can't forget it because I have to find another $1,000 to replace the $1,000 I lost by canceling your debt.

When God forgives sin He assumes responsibility for the sin Himself as well as releasing the forgiven sinner from all responsibility. The forgiven one may think it is "too easy," but for the Forgiver the cost was immeasurable—nothing less than personally accepting responsibility for the sin of the whole world, resulting in judgment of God. The cross is the point in human history where God not only clearly showed His willingness to release the debtors from all responsibility, but also He demonstrated His amazing readiness to assume full responsibility Himself.

The Debtor Must Accept the Forgiveness

Some people are too proud to accept anything they haven't earned. While we must admire their sense of integrity and their readiness to accept their full load of responsibility we must question their wisdom. Sooner or later we must admit that there comes a point in everyone's life where we need help. There is no such thing as the totally self-sufficient person. The time comes when we need a dentist or a plumber, a lawyer or a fireman. And when that time comes the sooner we admit our need and accept the help offered the better it will be for all concerned.

There is no avoiding the fact that we need the mercy and grace of God more than anything else in the world and to deny it is the most foolish action of which we are capable. To the self-made-man it is a humbling experience; to the self-sufficient woman it is a humiliating discovery. But like it or not, there must come a time when all are prepared by faith to receive from the Lord what we cannot and will not receive from any other source—the cancellation of

17

spiritual indebtedness! When this is accepted we can hear the words Jesus said to the woman in Simon's house, "Your sins are forgiven. . . . Your faith has saved you; . . . go in peace."

Simon was in bondage to his suspicious nature. He was bound by his need to conform to the norms of his society. Rules and regulations held him like a straitjacket. He had no alternative to his life of bondage for he thought that was how you did it. He had not discovered the extent of his indebtedness and so had no concept of the need for forgiveness. As a result he had to keep up with his rules, march to the beat of his regulations, hold his breath and look down his nose at everyone who thought otherwise.

The woman had a better approach. She had nothing to hide. She freely admitted what she was and deeply repented of what she had done. In Jesus she found the One who would accept responsibility for that which she could not handle, and from Him she heard the liberating words, "Your faith has saved you." She saw no necessity to conform to pharisaic rules to please God. There was in her mind no need to have a false evaluation of herself. She knew she was nothing more or less than a sinner saved by grace and to her everyone she ever met was in the identical position. Unless, of course, they were sinners not saved because they rejected grace.

Freed to Serve

The woman's freedom was not freedom to do what she pleased. It was freedom to do what her Forgiver pleased. She could never forget that He had assumed her debt. Not that He was going to hold it over her head as a means of extorting servile obedience, but rather that He had shown love to her beyond her comprehension and she loved Him because He had first loved her. So her new life was a life free from the bondage and tyranny of trying to please an implacable God and a critical society. It was a life where she was now free to kiss feet, express love, pour uninhibited gratitude and break the neck of any precious vase she possessed just as long as she lived a life that pleased Him.

There is no knowing what could happen in the church of Jesus Christ if those who attend could grasp the measure of their forgiveness, the magnitude of the debt Christ assumed, and the resultant sense of freedom. To be released into a life of uninhibited gratitude, with nothing to do but lovingly and lavishly please the Forgiver of their souls, would conceivably motivate and mobilize the forgiven people into such a life of worship and service that the world would be dumbstruck and awestruck with the sheer power of their witness and the quality of their lives.

2 Receptiveness— Is Anybody Listening?

Luke 8:4-15—The Sower

While a large crowd was gathering and people were coming to Jesus from town after town, he told this parable. "A farmer went out to sow his seed. As he was scattering the seed, some fell along the path; it was trampled on, and the birds of the air ate it up. Some fell on rock, and when it came up, the plants withered because they had no moisture. Other seed fell among thorns, which grew up with it and choked the plants. Still other seed fell on good soil. It came up and yielded a crop, a hundred times more than was sown."

When he said this, he called out, "He who has ears to hear, let him hear."

His disciples asked him what this parable meant. He said, "The knowledge of the secrets of the kingdom of God has been given to you, but to others I speak in parables, so that, 'though seeing, they may not see; though hearing, they may not understand.'

"This is the meaning of the parable: The seed is the word of God. Those along the path are the ones who hear, and then the devil comes and takes away the word from their hearts, so that they cannot believe and be saved. Those on the rock are the ones who receive the word with joy when they hear it, but they have no root. They believe for a while, but in the time of testing they fall away. The seed that fell among thorns stands for those who hear, but as they go on their way they are choked by life's worries, riches and pleasures, and they do not mature. But the seed on good soil stands for those with a noble and good heart, who hear the word, retain it, and by persevering produce a crop."

Jesus was sensational. Not that He was trying to be, He was simply endeavoring to communicate to His contemporaries what the Father had communicated to Him. But that was sensational!

For instance, when He talked about the Father and the existence they had shared "before the world was," that was sensational. And when He wanted to demonstrate the love and compassion of the Father to the needy by opening the eyes of the blind or putting together the twisted lives of the possessed, His miracles were sensational. Quite naturally He made enemies, for who could possibly challenge the power structures of the day as He did without incurring wrath and indignation. Yet the way He handled His enemies was nothing short of sensational. He routed them with ease!

A Diet of Mediocrity
People who live rather ordinary lives tend to sub-

sist on a diet of mediocrity. It comes as no surprise, therefore, that such people get excited about anything out of the ordinary that comes their way. Some years ago a researcher came up with a theory that the professional soccer teams in England were supported best by those who lived in dull surroundings. The color of the weekly event and the excitement of the contest was the only relief from the monotony and tedium which filled their lives. To a certain extent television has now made it possible for the bored and the lonely to have their sensations piped into their living rooms. This not only allows them to cope with a crippling sense of mediocrity and ordinariness, but it also gives them the chance to identify with exciting situations and glamorous people.

Recently, when my family and I were waiting to enter a restaurant, crowds of people began to gather because the Dallas Cowboys were staying in the hotel and were about to leave for their game with the Green Bay Packers. I was most interested to see how some of the people not only recognized the star players and the manager, but also felt free to go up to them, address them by their first names, and generally conduct themselves as if they were close friends, when in fact they had never met.

The Desire for Adventure

There is no doubt that people love those who can bring color and adventure to their lives. They make such people their heroes and establish them as personalities even to the point of feeling that they enjoy some special relationship.

This situation can be very difficult for the personalities who have a job to do. They may become so visible that they cannot move without attracting a crowd of well-wishers, hangers-on, and rippers-off.

Their ability to concentrate on their responsibilities is diminished and they may find it practically impossible to handle their own popularity.

Jesus would have understood the kind of tensions under which many "personalities" live because He went through the whole experience Himself. It was particularly difficult for Him because of the nature of His work.

There was no shortage of people eager to be part of the action that surrounded Jesus. The crowds flocked to hear the sensational things He said and to witness the sensational miracles He performed. But when He tried to make application, many of the people were not interested. Yet, His ministry was to reach the people at a level where deep transactions would be made. Without having the ear of the people He could not succeed; yet, at the same time, having their ears but not their willingness to obey and follow Him would not lead to His desired objective either.

His solution was to speak to the crowds in parables —engaging stories told in masterly fashion, greatly entertaining and enthralling. Those who wanted to be entertained and enthralled got what they wanted, but those who wanted to know God and experience His Kingdom in their lives were stimulated to think deeply, to dig out the underlying truth, and to inquire of the Master. This approach was demonstrated in striking fashion one day out in the open country as Jesus gathered the people around Him, quietened them, and told them the well-known story of the sower who sowed his field.

The Sower and the Seed

Sowers were to be seen over the hillsides as Jesus spoke. With their baskets full of seed, cradled under their left arms, they walked with easy grace throwing

23

handfuls of seed in an arc around their steps. The fields were traversed by paths worn hard by the feet of generations of villagers who had rights-of-way. As some of the seed fell on the path it was doomed to be snatched up by the hungry birds who wheeled and cried in pursuit of the sower. He was less than enthusiastic about feeding the birds with his precious seed, but there was little he could do about it except be as careful as possible.

The land was rocky with outcrops scattered over the hillside and a deficiency of deep soil over most of the area. It was hard for the sower to avoid throwing a certain amount of his seed on the rocky and stony areas. When he did, the seed was wasted because while shoots might spring up under the warm sunshine, they would not last long because of the lack of roots and the shortage of moisture.

In the cold winters the thorns would die off, but when the spring came along the warm weather would stir them into life and small thorn bushes would dot the landscape. If the seeds were sown in the place where the thorns would spring up they had no chance of survival because the strength of the thorn growth would choke the smaller, weaker shoots of grain.

With all these things against him it's a wonder the sower ever went out to sow his seed! But fortunately for him while there was a considerable amount of wasted seed there was always the possibility of a rich harvest, provided he could get the seed to fall on the good soil. In fact, while there were varying degrees of fertility in the soil of the area, there were some places where the remarkably fertile soil would produce bumper crops.

Revealed to Hearers Only

As Jesus talked about the sower to the crowds

there must have been something remarkably gripping about Him and the way He communicated because there would scarcely be a single person there who was not familiar with the troubles and hardships of the sowers and their farming operations. But He concluded His story with the challenging words, "He who has ears to hear, let him hear."

Back home, the disciples who had enjoyed the storytelling as much as the rest of the people recognized that the Master had something on His mind as He was telling the story and they knew that His final words meant that some would get the message and others would not. They wanted to make sure they got the message so they asked Him, "Would you explain the significance of the story, please?"

Jesus started by reminding the disciples of their privileged position. They had been granted the opportunities of hearing and understanding the "secrets of the kingdom of God." This meant that the things that God has in mind for the human race are not common knowledge for the simple reason that it takes more than street wisdom or university education to understand this kind of knowledge. In fact, the Scripture is careful to point out that the "secrets" are revealed to people who are prepared to be open to what God has to say. This does not mean that people put their minds out-of-gear, or check their intellect with their coats and umbrellas as they enter church, but rather that the Spirit of God reveals truth to people which they then work on with all the expertise and skill available. But behind all spiritual knowledge there must be spiritual revelation.

Other people, however, do not have this revelation. This was not a novel state of affairs in Christ's time. In fact, there have always been people devoid of truth as long as there have been people enriched by truth. Jesus quoted the prophet Isaiah who, in his time, could say, "Though seeing, they may not see; though hearing, they may not understand."

Hidden from Some

Some people feel that it is decidedly unfair of God to arbitrarily choose those who will have the revelation and those who will not. But it must be remembered that while it is true to say that God does make hearts hard and eyes blind and ears heavy, He does so only after there has been adequate opportunity for people to hear and see and understand. His action is, therefore, not an arbitrary action damning people to ignorance of God, but rather the action of One who has no desire to see His truth abused. Neither does He wish to irritate those who do not want to hear, or to harass those who have made up their minds they do not want to be serious about the things of the Kingdom. To God the things of the Kingdom are not for entertainment or debate, they are for deep belief and committed response. If this is not forthcoming, God refuses to allow His truth to be treated in the same way that pigs treat pearls that are thrown into the mud of their sty (see Matt. 7:6).

When Jehovah had His running conflict with Pharaoh concerning the release of the children of Israel, Pharaoh agreed to cooperate and then invariably "hardened his heart." God continued to work with him until one day something very terrible happened. *God* hardened Pharoah's heart! Pharaoh got God to cooperate in his own hardness when it became obvious that Pharaoh would not cooperate in God's plan of redemption.

In later years as Jesus stood before Pilate He responded to Pilate's questions with nothing more than a loud silence (see Mark 15:5).

Pilate had been exposed to the truth but had chosen to close his ears. This went on for some time until the Lord acted and closed Pilate's ears by the simple expedient of saying nothing to him. Pilate had got Christ to cooperate with him! From now on Pilate found it much easier to close his ears to Christ's words because there were no more words!

Slowly it dawned on the disciples that the Lord was not playing games even if many of the people were! He was deadly serious about what He was doing and He was not going to allow the people to miss the point of His ministry by thinking that He was simply there to bring a touch of glamour and excitement to their lives. As He explained the parable in detail to them this became increasingly clear.

The Seed Is the Word

"The seed is the word of God." Years later the beloved disciple would write in such a way that it was obvious that he regarded the Master as "the Word," but at the time Jesus was speaking to the disciples they may not have thought of the "word of God" in this fashion but rather as the prophets used the term. When the prophet in Old Testament times wished to impress the importance of his message upon his hearers he prefaced his remarks with the formidable words, "Hear the word of the Lord." This did not mean that God had uttered only one word but that He had made a statement which people needed to heed. In the spoken words of the prophets, which were often reinforced with dramatic actions, the people had the priceless opportunity of discovering what God had to say on a given subject. Later when Christ came in human flesh He added to the information which God had chosen to make available to the human race and in His life, death, and resurrection made a statement the like of which the world has never known. He is the Word!

Jesus was eager that His disciples should have a high view of God's revelation both in the spoken and the living word. It is doubtful if He could have achieved His objective in more masterful fashion than by using the disarmingly simple illustration of "seed" as "word."

For instance, *seed has the unique ability to contain life in seminal form while appearing to be dead in itself.* Take any dried-up seed and hold it in your hand. It will not jump or squeak, wriggle or squirm. It will just lie there until you let it slip and then it will stop where it drops. But don't be misled by this display of deadness, because the latent life within the husk has capabilities of reproduction and resources of power that defy comprehension.

Oak trees really do grow from acorns! Orchards can be developed from a handful of pips! So it is with the Word of God. To many it is dead. By the crowds it is ignored or scorned. In many homes it lies dead on a shelf holding faded photos, pressed flowers and genealogies of forgotten generations. But in individual lives it has brought about nothing short of revolution. Through the reading and heeding of the Word of God men have been saved from wrecking their lives and fragmenting their families. In lands across the sea, tribes have been won from their cannibalism, freed from their superstitions and introduced to lives of content and enrichment through the careful presentation of the Word of God. The seed is the Word!

Of course, the Word of God takes all kinds of abuse. I have spent many an hour talking to people who have never read what it has to say but have rejected what it says! They become quite agitated in their rejection of the Word of God! For years scholars have taken aim at the Word of God pointing out its "inaccuracies, inconsistencies, and contradictions" and many people think they have succeeded in robbing it of the authority wrongly placed upon it by segments of the church. But the Word is like seed.

Both word and seed have remarkable survival capabilities. Drop seed in a flood and it will float, leave it in ice and it will freeze, bury it in an Egyptian pyramid and it will stay in the dark. But take it from the flood, the frost, and the pyramid and give it some encouragement and it will get on with the business of reproducing itself. Both seed and the Word have stood the test of time and endured the onslaught of abuse without their latent powers being diminished.

Not all seed is sown by hand. Some is whipped away by the wind, some is transported on the wool of animals, some is even deposited in the droppings of birds, but it doesn't seem to mind. It just gets on with growing. I've been amazed at the resilience of the Word of God as it has been dispensed in so many ways. Preached from fashionable pulpits by eloquent, scholarly men to well-heeled congregations or explained in earthy terms to filthy men in skid row missions—it makes no difference. Communicated in the counseling room to the emotionally distraught, shared by the bed of the dying, discussed on campus by the earnest and the cynical—it works in all its power. In fact, it even appears to have the ability to survive the mistakes of those who minister it and bring blessing to some who don't even understand it!

This is not to suggest that the handling of the Word of God does not require the greatest care and preparation, but only to show that in itself the Word has seminal, survival, and dispersal capabilities that we do well to respect.

But when we finish saying all that can be said about seed we have to admit that without soil it doesn't amount to much. It takes seed and soil to produce the desired fruit.

The Soil Is the Human Being

Agriculture and animal husbandry account for 90 percent of the food needed to support the human race. Both agriculture and animal husbandry, however, depend entirely on soil to produce the nutrients that will supply the growth possibilities of crops. The human race would not survive without soil. This will come as a surprise to those of us whose only contact with soil is when we scrape it off the bottom of our boots before stepping on someone's Persian rug!

The soil has abilities to produce acids, gases, minerals; it acts as a reservoir for water, it breaks down injurious matter and releases it harmlessly into the atmosphere. It is responsible for maintaining an adequate supply of oxygen. And it does all this while we ignore it. The Encyclopaedia Britannica states that "one square meter of rich soil may contain more than one billion organisms" all of which are busy working and producing an environment in which the seed can be sown and the resultant life released.

Jesus did not say in so many words that the soil is the human being, but it is obvious from His parable that He was thinking this and it is easy to infer this from a study of what He said. So we are safe in saying that the potential of human beings to receive, as soil, the seed of the Word and be the means of releasing its life are monumental. When allowed to rest warmly in the mind of the scholar, the emotions of the artist, or the decision-making processes of the businessman, the possibilities of growth and nourishment for the human soil are clear for all to see.

When Augustine was wasting his life on dissolute living, his considerable mental abilities were dormant. But they were formidable, although no one would have benefited from them if the seed of the Word had not been planted. The musical genius of Handel was fertile soil as he worked and studied but his masterpiece "Messiah" was a result of the sowing of the Word in the soil of his creative genius.

But not all soil produces as it ought even when sown. This was the thrust of the parable of the sower. There was no doubt about the potential of both seed and soil but unless the soil came up to expectations even the superlative qualities of the seed would be squandered.

For instance, *the hard soil on the pathway through the fields* is an illustration of the kind of people whose minds are not receptive to the truth of God as it is on Christ. This does not necessarily mean that they are opposed to the Christian gospel. In fact, they may be "members in good standing" of respectable congregations, holding offices of ecclesiastical significance. But the Word which they hear regularly falls on their ears for no other reason than they are within range of the sound waves emanating from the mouth of the speaker and amplified through electronic equipment which cost the church a small fortune. Lying unheeded on the extremities of human consciousness, the Word is not allowed to lie there very long for "the devil comes and takes away the word from their hearts, so they cannot believe and be saved."

One of these days after you have attended church and heard the Word of God sown, stand in the foyer of the church and listen to the conversations of the people as they leave. You may be surprised how few will be discussing the things of God even though they have just been exposed to His Word. This can mean that the Word has fallen on unresponsive ground and the birds are busy snatching it away so quickly that there is a distinct possibility that the "hearers" will not remember a single thought within an hour. In all fairness, however, it must be said that many people who are good soil only get the chance to see their brothers and sisters at church and often need to visit with them or even transact some church business with them at that time.

The rocky soil represents those people who indicate great interest in the Word of God, particularly those parts of it which promise great blessing to them. When they hear it they respond with great joy and enthusiasm. And who can blame them for they are hearing the things they want to hear. They are being exposed to answers they have been seeking for a long time. But unfortunately these people were either only told half the message or they only hear half the message.

Unfortunately, in our enthusiasm to introduce people to God through His Word we shield the people from the parts they may not want to hear and we concentrate on the thing they may be anxious to hear. For instance, there are few people who will not be responsive to the invitation of our Lord, "Come to me, all you who are weary and burdened, and I will give you rest" (Matt. 11:28). The more weary and burdened the more likely they are to come to Him. But shortly after coming to Him they may discover that the weariness and the burden is the result of their own sin and if they are to find rest they must forsake the sin. They were not aware that the Lord said they should "take my yoke upon you and learn from me" (Matt. 11:29). Sad to say, there are many who respond to part of the message with great joy but disappear into the woodwork when confronted with the fulness of what Christ said. They are stony, rocky soil which does not produce the fruit from the seed.

The thorny soil represents the people who are open to the Word of God and give every indication that they are completely receptive to what the Lord has to say to them. But as the days go by it is apparent that they are not maturing in their relationship to the Lord. When you have time to sit down and talk to them you will discover that some conflict has arisen in their lives. A conflict between what they are primarily concerned about and what is of prime concern to the Lord. Accordingly, their minds have become captivated by "life's worries, riches and pleasures" and not with the things that God's Word says about these things. It is sad to see the fresh shoot of new life being choked by the thorny growth of weeds and thorns as these people show that their real concerns are secular rather than spiritual, and their orientation is earthly rather than heavenly.

If this picture is depressing let me remind you that if you keep sowing the seed you will eventually get some *into good soil* and the results will be most exciting and encouraging. There are some people who are so open and responsive to the Word of God that they receive it warmly, embrace it completely and begin to obey it wholeheartedly. They show every evidence of new life. Instead of careless indifference, they show careful attention to what God requires. In the place of instability and erratic behavior they grow in grace surely and persistently. They do not allow the thorns of secular influence and carnal thinking to overpower the fresh new shoots of life in Christ because they discipline themselves to weed and to cultivate the things of the Word in their lives.

To bring this parable right home we need to be reminded that we all have the privilege of being exposed to the Word of God and we all have the raw materials in our lives to provide the environment in which the truth of God can be released in our experience. The question is not whether the seed can do the job, however. The seed is good seed; it's the soil that is questionable. Many a critic of the preacher has sat in church evaluating the sower and the seed without realizing that what was actually happening was the seed was evaluating them, the soil. So "take heed how you hear."

3 Lovingness—The High Price of Neighborliness

Luke 10:25-37—The Good Samaritan

On one occasion an expert in the law stood up to test Jesus. "Teacher," he asked, "what must I do to inherit eternal life?"

"What is written in the Law?" he replied. "How do you read it?"

He answered: " 'Love the Lord your God with all your heart and with all your soul and with all your strength and with all your mind'; and, 'Love your neighbor as yourself.' "

"You have answered correctly," Jesus replied. "Do this and you will live."

But he wanted to justify himself, so he asked Jesus, "And who is my neighbor?"

In reply Jesus said: "A man was going down from Jerusalem to Jericho, when he fell into the hands of robbers. They stripped him of his clothes, beat him and went away, leaving him half dead. A priest happened to be going down the same road, and when he saw the man, he passed by on the other side. So too, a Levite, when he came to the place and saw him, passed by on the other side. But a Samaritan, as he traveled, came where the man was; and when he saw him, he took pity on him. He went to him and bandaged his wounds, pouring on oil and wine. Then he put the man on his own donkey, took him to an inn and took care of him. The next day he took out two silver coins and gave them to the innkeeper. 'Look after him,' he said, 'and when I return, I will reimburse you for any extra expense you may have.'

"Which of these three do you think was a neighbor to the man who fell into the hands of robbers?"

The expert in the law replied, "The one who had mercy on him."

Jesus told him, "Go and do likewise."

"How far is it to the sun, Dad?" asked the bright eyed eight-year-old.

"I'm sorry, son, I don't know," replied dad from behind the sports page.

"How hot is the sun, Dad?"

"What kind of a dumb question is that?"

Silence.

"Dad, how far is it from the center of the sun to the center of the moon?"

Dad, throwing down the paper answered grimly, "Son, I don't know how far it is from anywhere to the center of the moon."

"You don't care if I ask questions, do you, Dad?" insisted junior, totally oblivious to his dad's impatience.

Awkward pause.

"No son. How are you going to learn if you don't ask questions?"

Exactly. But not everyone who asks questions wants to learn and not everyone who is asked knows enough to teach.

Some people ask questions because they have a love affair with their own voice. Others simply want to display their knowledge. I remember being in a student meeting in Manchester University where a godly old minister was answering questions addressed to him by a hostile student body. After one insolent young man had asked a question which lasted approximately two minutes the minister peered over his glasses and said, "That was a statement. We are entertaining questions. Next question, please."

Sometimes the questioner thinks he can embarrass the person being questioned. This kind of approach is common in political rallies and open-air religious meetings. In "free for all" meetings of this nature there are always people who ask questions for which they desire no answers and upon which they hope to impale the unfortunate target of their questions.

Jesus had considerable experience in this kind of situation. One day an "expert in the law" listened impatiently to what He had to say and then posed the question, "Teacher, what must I do to inherit eternal life?" We are told that he wanted to "test" Jesus possibly by embarrassing, tripping, tricking or even discrediting Him. Yet at the same time it appears that he may have had a lingering desire to know the answer to the question. Perhaps like many people who ask such questions he was more interested in the answer than he cared to admit!

What Does the Law Require?

Recognizing that His questioner was "an expert in

the law" (someone well-versed not only in the law given to Moses but also in the vast network of technicalities that had been added to it over the years) Jesus answered him by asking him a question, one of Jesus' more effective and, to some people, infuriating techniques!

"You're an expert in the law. What does that law require you to do in order that you might inherit eternal life?"

"Love the Lord your God with all your heart and with all your soul and with all your strength and with all your mind and love your neighbor as yourself" the lawyer responded somewhat mechanically.

"That's right. If you do that you'll live." Obviously, by that statement the Lord equated "living" with an experience of a life of eternal quality on earth and a life of similar quality, without the distractions and limitations of earth, in heaven.

Seeing that he was neither ruffling Jesus' composure nor posing any difficulties to Him, the law expert became somewhat dissatisfied and embarrassed as the Lord pointed out to him that he already knew the answers to his own question. It became obvious that he was being either devious, stupid or both! So he tried to regain the initiative and salvage his dignity.

"Alright, you say I should love God wholeheartedly and love my neighbor as I love myself. But that doesn't say who is my neighbor."

At this point in the discussion Jesus told the parable of the Good Samaritan which is, without doubt, one of the world's superb short stories. Before we take time to examine it, however, we need to spend a little time thinking about the tremendous importance of neighborliness. It is noteworthy that God in His law, as revealed to Moses, should include love for neighbor in the same context as love for God. It is clear that His view of interpersonal relationships is considerably higher than that which is normative in contemporary society—or any other society for that matter!

Loving Neighbors Is Agreeing with God

Modern life makes great demands on people. This was brought home to me a couple of days ago when a close friend who is a successful surgeon examined my young son's ankle which had been injured in a basketball game. It became apparent that further examination and possible surgery was necessary so my surgeon friend began to make arrangements.

Unfortunately, as my wife and I began to look at our appointment book we could see only deadlines to be met, planes to be caught, interviews to be held— just a normal busy life stretching ahead of us! At that point, we were reminded of something that we had not exactly forgotten but were in danger of overlooking. In no uncertain terms my friend said, "Pete is more important than anything else tomorrow. Get him to the hospital whatever else goes by the board." In other words, people matter more than things!

God with all His multitudinous commitments has always made it clear that people have significance in His scheme of reckoning. That significance is derived from the fact that they were made by Him for a purpose devised by Him. To be more interested in things than people is to reverse the order of divine priority. But to see people as unique beings in God's economy and to put them in the place reserved for them by God is to agree with God on a basic fact of human existence. To disregard, use, manipulate, abuse or destroy people is in disagreement with God's standards and to be out-of-step with His purposes.

Loving Neighbors Is Loving as God Loves

Loving is not ignoring. Neither is it tolerating. The right attitude to neighbors has to be much more than an occasional "hi" as one rider-mower rider passes another close to the invisible boundaries between suburban plots. Neither is it the annual push-out-of-the-ditch when the first snows of winter catch the unprepared unawares! To love neighbors is to have, at least, the kind of concern for people that individuals have for their own well-being.

Each individual has minimally a concern for his own safety, comfort, and freedom (to name only a few personal concerns). To love the neighbor is to be concerned about these factors in another person's life—not in a technical or academic sense, but in an involved, practical sense. The obvious practicality of God's love for people is seen to greatest advantage in the events of the Incarnation and Crucifixion. The human plight so clearly recognized by God was neither ignored nor merely a cause for concern, but a call to action. An action requiring nothing less than the assumption of the frailties and frustrations of human flesh and the endurance of the ignominy and agony of human rejection and crucifixion.

Loving Neighbors Is Obeying God

It is remarkable that God should make so few demands on human beings. All His requirements are summed up in "love God and love your neighbor." As Jesus pointed out repeatedly, this says it all. It is difficult for us to accept so simple and fundamental a blueprint for human behavior, particularly as we discover more of the complexities of human nature and the intricacies of human society. Yet the statement stands on its own merits and, notwithstanding all mankind's attempts to ignore or substitute them, there is no doubt that this is the way to go. One must realize that when politicians make their pitches and philosophers air their theses and sociologists publish their findings, they are all saying that if humanity is to flourish and society is to survive then "love" is the only means whereby these noble ends can be achieved. They do not, of course, use theological language or indulge in biblical quotations, but a keen listener will recognize the reality behind the rhetoric and discern the substance shrouded in the statistics.

To many people it will come as a surprise that God was right after all, and unfortunately for some, the realization comes only after the total collapse and merciless routing of their alternative approaches to life. It is, however, at this point that we must recognize that while God did give man the freedom to obey or disobey His commands, He did not offer humanity alternative approaches to life. He said that we could do it His way and live, or not do it His way and die. But He did not say "the following are the various options open to you for living your lives." Accordingly, to love God and neighbor is not one of the ways of living, it is the only way of living. To not love God and neighbor is to choose to die.

Not Loving Neighbors Is Sin

To recognize that neighbor-love is a requirement, not an option, and to see that neighbor-love is an attitude of self-giving related to the self-giving of God in Christ is to be confronted with the seriousness of loving neighbors. We don't like to confront serious things or to be confronted by them. One man was worried by newspaper articles showing the relationship between smoking and lung cancer and he became so upset with the information that he knew he had to do something about it. He cancelled his newspaper! Another man when confronted by fellow believers with the fact that his adultery was sin, knew that he must take some action. He did—he left the church and started his own church! The legal expert when confronted by Jesus with the importance of neighbor-love knew that he had not measured up to the divine requirement or obeyed the divine command. Rather than admit it, however, he took evasive action. "Who is my neighbor?" he asked, no doubt thinking that if he could get Christ to debate him on the subject he might be able to put up a smoke screen and make good his escape.

My experience has been that people try to joke themselves out of the situation. "You should see my neighbor!" or "I sure could love my neighbor's wife —have you seen her?—but my neighbor—that's another subject!" Or, "If God would give me a new set of neighbors I'll be glad to see what I can do about loving them!" All very amusing, but God is not amused. To pull these kinds of lines is as well advised as to try to joke your way out of court or try to avoid a conviction by making some facetious remarks or hilarious offers to a federal judge.

To love neighbors is divine law. Not to love neighbors is law-breaking—law breaking is sin—sin is not a joke! When Paul wrote that "through the law we became conscious of sin" (Rom. 3:20), he was telling us, among other things, that we can measure our sinfulness by our lack of neighbor-love. Once aware of our sinfulness we can look for forgiveness through God's gracious offer of salvation in Christ, and hence inherit eternal life.

So we can enjoy eternal life two ways. First, by living a life of consistent, unfailing love for God and neighbor which, of course, is possible only in theory, but beyond the ability of sinful mankind in practice.

Second, through recognizing our sinfulness through our lack of neighborliness and coming repentantly to Christ for forgiveness and the gift of eternal life. That is why neighbors are not a joke, and neighborliness is not a subject for debate. It is a life and death matter! This soon became apparent to the lawyer as Jesus told His story.

Who Is My Neighbor?

The road from Jerusalem to Jericho is a steep rugged descent through inhospitable countryside that, in Christ's day, was infested with bands of robbers. For someone to be attacked and robbed on that journey would probably be as commonplace as unwary visitors to New York being mugged at night in Central Park. This is not to minimize the sufferings of either the unfortunate Jerusalem traveler or the New York visitor, but to point out once again the extraordinary skill with which Jesus took the commonplace and invested it with uncommon significance.

The plight of the unfortunate victim was serious. Left half-dead in such an environment he would soon be 100 percent dead through exposure and thirst unless promptly cared for. This was perfectly clear to the legal man whose question, "Who is my neighbor?" had prompted the story. To be aware of need and alert to opportunities to meet need does not necessarily mean that those who are in position to help will help.

The priest—a representative of the worship of God —came by the scene of the brutal attack, saw the man in the ditch and didn't even cross the road to check his condition. We have no way of knowing what was going through his mind but we do know what was not flowing through his veins! Perhaps he had a commitment to another sick person, a funeral, a wedding, a board meeting. Perhaps he didn't feel well or he was just scared or he just didn't want to get involved. We don't know, but we recognize the attitude and sense something of the shame of the situation when we remember the needy we have passed by on the other side.

The priest was followed by a Levite who was equally aware of the situation. He also had an equal responsibility to minister to the man in the ditch and failed equally to behave in a way that showed a degree of understanding for the divine command to "love your neighbor as yourself." By their action—or lack of action—both priest and Levite demonstrated their ignorance of the worth of a person made in God's image, and the magnitude of their sin in disobeying God's Word even though they were nominally committed to the service of God and man.

The answer to the question was now perfectly clear. Your neighbor is the man in the ditch! He is the man who can't do anything for himself or for you; he is the one you don't know; he is the one whose condition nauseates you; he is the one who can't possibly appreciate you or repay you; he may not even recognize you. Quite possibly, he will not survive his ordeal in order to thank you. So that's who your neighbor is and this is what neighborliness is?

Neighborliness is getting to the unpleasant and helpless and ministering to them without even a thought of reward or thanks or appreciation. Of course, these may be forthcoming, but if they are, they will be a pleasant surprise not the fulfilling of your "unalienable right."

The Good Samaritan

Samaritans and Jews didn't get along. In fact, when

Jesus met the Samaritan woman she said that "they had no dealings" with each other (see John 4:9). There aren't many Samaritans left now but the two groups still have their problems. This is partly because the Jews regard them as inferior half-breeds—the product of ancient alliances not acceptable to God—and the Samaritans, of course, are offended by this attitude. The Samaritans were the despised people in Jewish society so were probably the butts of ethnic jokes and the recipients of grudging hand-outs and nothing more.

The scathing irony of Christ's story would not be lost on His questioner even if it is somewhat lost on us. To be told that a despised Samaritan would function correctly in the situation in which both the Levite and priest had failed, was to be told something most unpalatable.

The Samaritan "had pity" on the stranger and having pity became a very costly exercise. I don't suppose he was carrying a first-aid kit so in all probability the bandages he used were his ripped up garment; the oil and the wine he poured in the wounds were intended for some other more joyous use. Putting the man on his donkey meant either throwing some of his goods away to make room for him, or giving the wounded man his own seat. Either way, it was a costly involvement. Going to the inn—the ruins of which are still to be seen on the roadside—and checking in the stranger, paying his rent, and committing himself to any further expense all pointed to a willingness to be neighborly to the point of hurting.

The Price of Neighborliness

Sometimes if we are confronted with our own lack of neighborliness we feel guilty and take immediate action. We decide that we will do something about our neighbors not according to their need but according to what we are prepared to do for them. This can lead us to the ridiculous situation where we find people doing things for others that they neither need nor want while refusing to do the things that really are needed. It's more fun doing what is fun than doing what is needed!

The Samaritan could have addressed the half-dead man in the ditch and said, "Here's two denarii, go and get a drink or you'll die of thirst." Or if his interest was music he might have suggested that when the man felt better he should give him a call and they could have a meal together and then go to hear the Samaritan Symphony.

Neighborliness operates at the peculiar point of need of the neighbor, not at the special point of interest of the donor.

Go and Do Likewise

"Which of these three do you think was a neighbor to the man who fell into the hands of robbers?" asked the Master.

"The one who had mercy on him," replied the lawyer without hesitation.

Jesus told him, "Go and do likewise."

It should be clear to all of us that the lawyer got a lot more than the answer to his question. He learned that his neighbor was the man in the ditch, that neighborliness costs and hurts, and that some people who are held in high esteem in the religious world know little or nothing about the practicalities of neighborliness, while some despised people are experts. But more than anything else he was told to, "Go and do something." Once he had been shown what neighborliness is and once his neighbor had been clearly identified all that remained for him to do was to stop

46

asking smart questions and start doing some smart acts of love.

I have no doubt that all of us need the same message. Some of us who are pleased with our moral integrity and social acceptability need to be told to practice love for God and neighbor so that we can be stripped down to the bare inadequacies of our own self-righteousness that we might come to repentance. Others of us who have been saved need to be reminded that once saved by grace through faith we are to live in the power of the spirit and produce the "righteousness of the law," which is a loving attitude to God and neighbor.

Neighborliness in Church

Surely the place where neighborliness should be more in evidence than any other place on earth is in the church of Jesus Christ. Those who are redeemed by the blood of Christ have learned to love the people in the ditch. They are prepared to love till it hurts. They expect to be involved even when it costs and they do it not for reward or acknowledgement but for love of the One who saved them and out of love for those He loves.

4 Prayerfulness— A Persistent Knocking

Luke 11:1-13—A Friend at Midnight

One day Jesus was praying in a certain place. When he finished, one of his disciples said to him, "Lord, teach us to pray, just as John taught his disciples."

He said to them, "When you pray, say: 'Father, hallowed be your name, your kingdom come. Give us each day our daily bread. Forgive us our sins, for we also forgive everyone who sins against us. And lead us not into temptation.'"

Then he said to them, "Suppose one of you has a friend, and he goes to him at midnight and says, 'Friend, lend me three loaves of bread, because a friend of mine on a journey has come to me, and I have nothing to set before him.'

"Then the one inside answers, 'Don't bother me. The door is already locked, and my children are with me in bed. I can't get up and give you anything.' I tell

you, though he will not get up and give him the bread because he is his friend, yet because of the man's persistence he will get up and give him as much as he needs.

"So I say to you: Ask and it will be given to you; seek and you will find, knock and the door will be opened to you. For everyone who asks receives; he who seeks finds; and to him who knocks, the door will be opened.

"Which of you fathers, if your son asks for a fish, will give him a snake instead? Or if he asks for an egg, will give him a scorpion? If you then, though you are evil, know how to give good gifts to your children, how much more will your Father in heaven give the Holy Spirit to those who ask him!"

Jesus was committed to prayer. In the midst of His hectic schedule of traveling and ministering He made sure that He didn't miss His prayer time. Conscious as He was of the appalling human need on every hand He did not feel obligated to spend all His waking hours meeting the needs and demands of the people, nor did He hesitate to withdraw from the crowds and spend time in solitude and communion with the Father. In fact, He impressed upon His followers the absolute necessity for solitude, withdrawal, prayer and spiritual refreshment.

One of the disciples observed the Lord's quiet experiences. One time, after waiting for Him to conclude, he asked if it would be possible to have some lessons in prayer. Evidently, the disciple was convicted by the example of His Master and had a desire to improve his own prayer experience. He was also aware that John the Baptist had spent time showing his men how to pray.

Jesus was perfectly happy to accede to His disci-

49

ple's request and outlined to him the prayer we commonly call "The Lord's Prayer." It is probable that the disciple was already familiar with this prayer as the Lord apparently had already taught it to His disciples and expressed a desire that they use it regularly. Not in a mechanical repetitious sense (a style of praying He disliked and discouraged) but more as a guide to the fundamental aspects of prayer which they should never forget.

Pray ... Father

"When you pray," Jesus said, "Pray ... Father." Prayer involves asking, and the important thing about asking is that you ask the right person.

Jesus demanded an intimacy of relationship with the transcendent God which could only be known by those who had come to Him humbly and repentantly and found in Him mercy and grace. This relationship, in Jesus' case, had been preserved from eternity because sin had never entered in. But in the disciples' case, and in ours, relationship was restored because their sins, and ours, have been blotted out. Accordingly, the disciples came to God in prayer and addressed Him adoringly as "Father," just as we do.

In the presence of the living, loving God who we know as Father, disciples have a great sense of gratitude and appreciation for who God is. This appreciation is mixed, however, with sorrow that the Father is not appreciated as He ought to be by other people. Accordingly, the initial request and heart desire of the praying disciple is that the "name"—that is the Being of God—might be "hallowed" or respected. In other words, prayer starts with concern for the honor of the Father rather than the requests of the Father's children.

There is also a consciousness that the Father is

working in His universe in general, and on earth in particular in order that His supreme reign might be recognized and acknowledged from star to shining star. Disciples know that one day the history of earth and man will come to a great and glorious climax when every knee will bow to Jesus Christ and every tongue will confess Him as Lord (see Rom. 14:11) in such a way that the Father will be glorified. To this end Jesus taught His disciples to pray.

A follower of Christ is one who is disenchanted with the condition of this world and looking forward to something totally different in the new and glorious Kingdom. Not that we are unrelated to our present environment, or living lives strangely detached from reality. On the contrary, we are to be so in tune with reality and so aware of our situation that we can see the ways in which the Kingdom is already being established in individuals and communities, and we are combining our endeavors with the workings of God in the Kingdom-building process.

Daily Bread

With the glory and the Kingdom of God as their main concerns, Jesus was perfectly happy to have His disciples share with the Father some of their more mundane concerns, like what they were going to have for lunch and where they were going to sleep that night!

"Daily bread" belongs on the prayer agenda because the Father is concerned that those who serve Him be adequately equipped for such service. Without meeting basic need it is not possible for human beings to function properly. God knows that better than anyone, seeing He built in the need and supplied the answers so there should be no reticence on the part of disciples when it comes to praying about our needs being met. The operative word, of course, is "need." Without drawing too much out of the prayer we should note that He said "daily bread" not vichyssoise, chateaubriand, avec champignons, fromage, cafe au lait, champagne.

Need and want should be clearly distinguished and great care should be taken to pray for the one and to treat the other with considerable circumspection.

Forgiven and Forgiving

The prayer that Jesus taught His disciples also reminded them constantly of their own sinfulness and the necessity for ongoing repentance and confession. Initial forgiveness is available to all who come to Christ in repentance and faith, but ongoing cleansing is necessary as disciples learn to walk more closely to their Lord. In fact, the closer we get to Him and the more we endeavor to walk in His ways, the more we become aware of our failings and shortcomings. There is no inconsistency, therefore, in the Christian teaching that we are both forgiven and need to go on being forgiven because we were sinners and we go on being sinners.

Some confusion has been generated by the statement, "Forgive us our sins, for we also forgive everyone who sins against us."

Cursory reading of this has led some people to feel that God will forgive them because they are forgiving others. Two things need to be made clear at this point. First, if we are only forgiven in the degree that we are forgiving, there are precious few forgiven people around! Second, Scripture is careful to point out that our salvation and all that is incorporated in it is the result of God's grace not our worth. If I could say I deserve to be forgiven because I forgave my brother, then my salvation would be a result of my activity which, of course, is contrary to the teaching of Scripture.

What then does this expression teach? It teaches that as forgiven sinners come to the Father for continual cleansing and forgiveness they do so in a forgiving attitude. They are not forgiven because they are forgiving. They have learned to be forgiving because they have experienced the inexpressible joy of being forgiven. The forgiving life-style is a grateful response to the grace of God, not a puny attempt to merit the favor of God.

Testing for Maturity

It is interesting to notice that the disciples, whom many modern Christians treat as supermen and position on pedestals, would never have agreed to such treatment because they certainly didn't see themselves in such light. They were all too aware of their sinfulness and conscious of their own susceptibility to failure and defeat. Testing came their way with relentless regularity and they knew that they were easy meat for many of the things that confronted them.

The disciples recognized that their Lord would not forsake them and they realized that the testings that came their way always bore the stamp of His approval. They also had no doubt that He approved the testing, not because He enjoyed seeing them squirm, but in order that they might come through the experience stronger and more mature in their faith. But they still didn't like the testing any more than we do and they didn't trust themselves any more than we should! So they were encouraged to pray to the Father, "Lead us not into temptation."

Prayer and Persistence

The response of the Lord to His disciple's request

may have been somewhat disappointing, particularly if the disciple had already been praying the prayer on a regular basis. He might have felt that the Lord was repeating Himself and not really getting to the point of teaching him how to pray. But he was due for a surprise! As soon as He finished repeating the prayer, the Lord launched straight into a story about a friend who had a friend who had a friend!

Friend number one had gone to bed for the night when his friend, who had a habit of traveling late at night, arrived on the doorstep looking tired and hungry. Friend number one was glad and sad to see his friend. Glad because he was a friend, sad because his cupboard resembled "old Mother Hubbard's" cupboard. Excusing himself, he hurried across the street to the home of another friend who had also gone to bed. By this time it was midnight and, realizing it was late, friend number one knocked loudly on the door even though he knew he wouldn't be too popular. He was right. Sticking his head out of the window friend number three hissed, "What's going on? Don't you know what time it is? You'll wake the baby after we've struggled to get him to go to sleep. Go away!"

Friend number one cupped his hands around his mouth and stage-whispered, "Hey, it's me. I'm sorry to bother you but I need some bread right now. Come on down and get it for me. The sooner you do it the sooner you can get back to sleep." Friend number three, when he realized who it was and why he had come, promptly came downstairs, tripped over the cat, stubbed his toe on the dresser, but managed a grin as he handed over the bread. "Thanks," smiled friend number one. "Sweet dreams!"

Attitude of Prayer

This touching humorous story seems at first to be

out of place in a talk on prayer until we remember that attitude is a major part of praying effectively. There was a confidence about the friend who woke the other friend at midnight that spoke well of the relationship they enjoyed. He didn't really mind going to his house at midnight because he knew his friend would help at any time. He didn't mind waking him up either because he knew that while his neighbor might be a little grumpy, he would get over it as soon as he realized the need.

One of the nice things about friendship is the confidence it gives you to make all manner of requests of your friend. If a stranger comes up to me and asks to borrow my car I would be inclined to say, "Do you know any more jokes." But if a close friend comes and asks I would be pleased he asked and delighted to help.

Confidence in Prayer

It is important to know that prayer based on the right kind of relationship with the Father breeds confidence. The story is not intended to show God as a grumpy old gentleman whose sleep is disturbed every time one of His children has an emergency. The intention of the story is to portray the attitude of family relationship and undaunted confidence that disciples ought to have when they approach the Father in prayer.

Another reason for confidence in prayer is that God is totally reliable. Most children learn to trust their fathers when they are very young and, while there are unfortunate exceptions, most fathers revel in the obvious trust with which their children approach them. It is conceivable that there may be some weird, demented men who would give their children snakes when they asked for fish, and some hardhearted old skinflints may, for reasons known only to themselves, hand over a stone to their youngster instead of some bread. But the heavenly Father would never do anything so ghoulish or so heartless.

Provided we need a fish we can expect to receive a fish from the Father. There will be no hidden fangs, no disguised traps, no subtle catches, just straightforward answers to prayer. If it is bread we need then we can anticipate bread. There is no such thing as a useless stone being sent from the Father when His children need bread. He would not stoop to do anything as thoughtless as to fail His children. God is committed to doing nothing less than meeting the bona fide needs of His disciples.

The disciple who wanted to learn how to pray would, by this time, have learned a lot that would stand him in good stead in days to come. Not only had he been reminded of the One to whom he should pray and the things about which it was perfectly legitimate to pray but, through the story of the friends, he had been shown that where real friendship exists and genuine family concerns are in evidence, then people can be confident that the one who is being asked for help can be counted on to respond positively. This assurance is the bedrock on which confident expectation is built.

Having illustrated this, Jesus went on to explain to His disciple how he could realistically approach the Father. He was told to ask, seek and knock, and promised that if he asked he would be given, if he sought he would find, and if he knocked the door would swing open.

Asking

We know from James that it is possible "to ask with wrong motives" (see Jas. 4:3); we have only the

56

gratification of our own selfishness in mind when we make a request. The Father does not promise to grant positive answers to some of our requests because, while we may think that we are asking for fish, what we may be desiring would be a serpent if granted; and our system of values can be so confused that what we imagine to be bread could be as worthless as a stone and just as heavy around our necks. To be promised a positive reply to all our requests, therefore, can mean a positive answer in a form that we do not immediately recognize.

When my family and I were making arrangements to move from England to the United States we had to apply for a special Residential Alien Visa. We prayed that God would grant that we might receive the visa as quickly as posible so that the work of the church could go on unhindered. We felt that we were making a legitimate request for the sake of the Kingdom and we knew we were asking the Lord to grant something that would expedite the outworking of His revealed will to us. But that did not mean that the visa came sailing through. In fact, delay followed delay until many months elapsed before we were able to make the trans-Atlantic flight and embark on our new ministry.

The disappointment caused by the delay was hard and the uncertainty of our situation was very unsettling both for the church and our family. But soon after we arrived in our new ministry we realized how invaluable the delay had been both on our family preparations and the advantage for the church in being without a pastor for a period of time. Personally, we were asking God for bread in our understanding which, if granted as requested, would have been a stone! It's great to know that God will give what we ask even if we don't always know what we are asking.

Seeking

How often should you pray for a certain thing? Some people are of the opinion that if you really trust God you only need to mention the request to Him once. As He is neither deaf nor forgetful it is not necessary to repeat yourself. Others point to the fact that Paul prayed three times about his thorn in the flesh and Jesus, in the Garden of Gethsemane, prayed more than once about the possible removal of the impending agony. There is also little doubt that the prayer we have been thinking about in this chapter was designed to be repeated so I advise people that they may feel perfectly comfortable repeating a request to the Lord.

Related to this concern is the confusion that exists in some people's minds about the legitimacy of taking any steps to effect the results of prayer. For instance, a young man who has prayed about a certain young lady yet feels he should not take any steps to meet the object of his affection, is presumably trusting God to do something miraculous. While the degree of trust exhibited in such a case must be applauded I feel that the confidence may well be misplaced, for God certainly has given us capabilities and responsibilities for undertaking practical action. I believe this is what the Lord had in mind when He said we should not only "ask" but also "seek."

Certainly we should be relating our concerns in prayer to the Lord, but we should also be taking steps to explore the possibilities of answers to prayer through responsible action. So I would encourage this young man to keep on praying but also to remember that a "faint heart never won a fair lady" and he should seek an opportunity to get together with her rather than wait for the Lord to deliver her to him in some miraculous fashion!

Knocking

As is the case with the words "ask" and "seek" the instruction to "knock" is a present imperative which means, literally, that disciples should go on asking, seeking and knocking. This word is obviously used metaphorically and probably means that we should exhibit a sincere tenacity. To knock on a door is to demonstrate a desire to meet with whatever is inside and to continue knocking is to show that there is some degree of urgency about the desire. Desultory praying and disinterested praying are, therefore, ruled out. To pray confidently and effectively requires an attitude that gets results from a loving Father through continued reiteration of desire, and practical involvement in exploring all lines of possible answers.

Good Gifts

The great climax to the story told by Jesus to His questioning disciple came when He said, "Fathers know how to give good gifts to their children so you can be confident that the Father will give the Holy Spirit to those who ask Him." It would appear from this statement that the answering of prayer is basically a spiritual experience with practical application. It is the Holy Spirit who is made real to praying people in response to their asking, seeking and knocking. This is, no doubt, hard to understand if you have been asking for a girl friend and finish up with a Holy Spirit experience! But when we consider the Holy Spirit as the greatest of all gifts and see Him included in the practical things that we receive from the Lord, we understand the greatness of answered prayer.

If you were asking for a girl friend and the Lord led you to the woman of His choice (and you agreed!) don't forget the work of the Spirit in the love, joy, and peace you found in the relationship. If, however, you asked for a certain thing and the answer was "no" and you realized that it would have been a serpent or a stone if delivered as you had ordered, don't forget the way in which you experienced the Holy Spirit in terms of long-suffering, faithfulness and gentleness in the situation!

5 Generousness— An Investment in Eternity

Luke 12:13-21—The Rich Fool

Someone in the crowd said to him, "Teacher, tell my brother to divide the inheritance with me."

Jesus replied, "Man, who appointed me a judge or an arbiter between you?" Then he said to them, "Watch out! Be on your guard against all kinds of greed; a man's life does not consist in the abundance of his possessions."

And he told them this parable: "The ground of a certain rich man produced a good crop. He thought to himself, 'What shall I do? I have no place to store my crops.'

"Then he said, 'This is what I'll do. I will tear down my barns and build bigger ones, and there I will store all my grain and my goods. And I'll say to myself, "You have plenty of good things laid up for many years. Take life easy; eat, drink and be merry." '

"But God said to him, 'You fool! This very night

61

*your life will be demanded from you. Then who will
get what you have prepared for yourself?'*

*"This is how it will be with anyone who stores up
things for himself but is not rich toward God."*

Many preachers spend a considerable amount of
time preparing their sermons before they stand before the people on the Lord's Day. They diligently
search the Scriptures to find out what God wants to
say to His people through them. Searching their own
hearts they pray and work hard to be prepared as
God's spokesmen to the people for whom they are
responsible. When the great day comes they stand
before the people to deliver their souls. With voices
throbbing with intensity, eyes aflame with zeal, ges-
ticulating, exhorting, encouraging and reproving they
bring the word of the Lord to the people and lift the
people to the worship of God.

That's how it is supposed to work! But many
people who have devoted themselves to ministry
know that "it ain't necessarily so." I used to be extremely frustrated when I would preach my heart out
then find that the people didn't seem to realize what
was going on. For instance, after "delivering my
soul" one day on the "Attributes of God" with the
intention of elevating people's thought from the mundane to the spiritual, I was delighted to see people
standing in line to talk to me. But the more I talked
to them the more frustrated I became. The first two
people wanted to know if I would marry them next
Saturday. The next lady and her husband wanted to
know what to do about their son who was in prison.
They were followed by a lady who had just received
divorce papers and she gave way to an irate gentleman who was upset about his son being disciplined in
the Sunday School hour!

Because of my attitude I am sure that I did not deal with their problems as well as I ought and when it was all over I thought seriously about the whole situation. Were the people living on a different wave length than I? Were they listening to me at all? Was the Word of God getting through to them? Were we as a church becoming so involved in human need that we were in danger of losing sight of God or was I becoming so wrapped up with God that I was no longer able to relate to people? Had I arrived at the point of being so heavenly minded that I was no earthly use, or were some of the people so earthly minded they were of no heavenly use?

Subsequently, I was greatly encouraged to discover not only that all preachers go through this kind of thing, but that the Lord Himself had the same problem. One day when He was surrounded by milling crowds of people He took the opportunity to teach His disciples, presumably with the crowd of people listening in. He got into some very heavy subjects such as hypocrisy, hell, the count God keeps of people's hairs, the unforgiven sin, and what to do when persecuted. It is hard to imagine how He began to deal with all these important matters without teaching a Bible school course, but apparently He managed and many of the people were immeasurably helped and challenged by the things He said.

Where There's a Will ...

There was, however, somewhere in the crowd a little man who was not remotely interested in all the things that were being taught. It would be natural to assume that he left early, but strange as it may seem he stayed under the sound of the Master's voice even though the message was not registering at all. He had a problem which so gripped his attention that he could think of nothing else and like the people who came to speak with me after the talk on the "Attributes of God," he waited to talk to the Lord about his concern. "Teacher, tell my brother to divide the inheritance with me," he said.

When I was young I was told, "Where there's a will there's a way." But when I grew older I discovered it is more accurate to say, "Where there's a will there's a quarrel!" Evidently, the man and his brother had lost a loved one who had left them a sum of money. The other man had found a way to keep both his own share and that of his brother, a state of affairs that had understandably upset the man who spoke out at the meeting. To say that he was upset would be to put it mildly! Having tried all that he knew he decided to bring the matter up in public.

In our hometown we have a television station which runs a news feature called Contact 6. The idea behind Contact 6 is that there are a lot of people who are dissatisfied with the products they have bought in the marketplace or the services that have been rendered to them. Many of these people have tried to get refunds or repairs from the people with whom they have done business but without any success. At that point they are invited to contact Contact 6, explain their problem and leave it to the newsman to see what can be done about it. He, armed with a camera crew, visits the place of business and endeavors to get the matter settled on camera if at all possible. There is something about seeing a big businessman squirm and a little man triumphantly waving a check that makes hundreds of people watch with great glee and, of course, the television station watches the ratings with great glee. In fact, there's glee all around except in the offices of the businessman.

It may be that the man in the crowd decided to use

the Lord Jesus in much the same way. His reasoning was quite simple: "I can't get my brother to pay me my share, but if I bring it up in front of the crowd and get the Teacher to tell him to pay up I should get the money out of him even if he only pays up out of embarrassment." But he was due to be disappointed! "Man, who appointed me a judge or an arbiter between you?" answered the Lord. "What makes you think that I'm here to settle disputes between people who ought to be perfectly capable of settling their own disputes. I have more important things to do than to get involved in matters of such relative unimportance!"

Be on Your Guard

The Master's answer raises a very interesting point. Did He not regard such matters as the one raised by the disgruntled brother important and, if so, was He removed from the real concerns and problems of the people to whom He had come to minister? I think the answer is that He was certainly concerned about the things that worried people, but He was more concerned about giving the people spiritual principles which they themselves should apply rather than arbitrate in every situation that came up in the turbulent lives of the people around Him. In fact, I think we can see this very clearly by His next statement. "Watch out! Be on your guard against all kinds of greed; a man's life does not consist in the abundance of his possessions." In other words, Jesus knew the man's problem better than the man himself. Accordingly, He addressed Himself to the real concern rather than the apparent concern.

Like the good physician that He was, He started to treat disease rather than symptoms. The disease that both brothers were suffering from was greed. The man who had kept his brother's share was greedy, and the man who had lost his share was also so greedy that he could think about nothing else. Even to the point of being incapable of concern about such things as hypocrisy and hell, persecution and perseverance, the sin of blasphemy against the Holy Spirit, which will not be forgiven, and the protection of God's children which will never be broken.

Having shocked his interrupter into silence and, no doubt, having gained the attention of all the people around Him the Master immediately seized the moment and told one of His superb parables.

Visions of Plenty

"There was a farmer who was so skilled and so successful that he had a problem resulting from his success. He was producing such bumper crops that he couldn't store them and this was causing him much concern. He thought long and hard about the problem and came to a decision that was both sound and courageous. Rather than rest on his oars or deal half-heartedly with his problem, he determined to take the major step of tearing down his existing barns and totally rebuilding. To have added to his barns would have produced no long-range solution. His only hope was to go into a major rebuilding program and make the large capital investment the program would require, and then settle back and live on the results.

"The more he thought about it the more excited he became. Visions of plenty and thoughts of many years of prosperous ease crowded into his mind. I'll 'take life easy; eat, drink, and be merry,' he thought. But he had not reckoned with someone who had been reading his unspoken thoughts with interest and examining his unpublished plans with great concern. This One spoke up and said, 'You fool! This very night your life will be demanded from you.' "

Dying had never entered the farmer's mind! Life seemed to stretch away to unlimited horizons. The things he had earned and the fruits of his labors, the life-style he enjoyed and the prospects he dreamed about were his only concerns. The thought of death had never occurred to him. And the thought of having to leave all that he had worked for was unthinkable. Leaving all that he had earned? Leaving it all to someone who had not earned it? Leaving it all and having to live without it? Unthinkable thoughts—that was why he had never entertained them. But when God spoke to him and delivered the announcement concerning the termination of the only life he knew and the only life-style he had entertained, he was shattered. And that is the exact position of every person who lives for his material possessions and ignores spiritual realities. That is the position of those whose lives are governed by greed.

Greed Always Wants More

If it is possible that greed can blind a person's eyes to such realities as death and dull people's conscience to other people's need, it is evident that greed ought to be a matter of prime concern. We live in an age where some live comfortably with abundance while giving little or no thought to the millions who lack the bare necessities.

Our generation, like preceding generations, demonstrates its greed in every echelon of society. The Communists sneer at the Capitalists insisting that "Free Enterprise" operates solely on the principle of greed, while the Capitalists take great delight in pointing out the inequities in the Communist societies where the privileged classes show they have the identical problem.

The boardrooms of big business constantly bemoan the greed of the unions which, of course, insist on getting a "fair share" of profits out of the pockets of greedy management and even more greedy stockholders.

Politicians vote themselves raises while asking the people to engage in voluntary wage restraint while the people know perfectly well that if they voluntarily restrain themselves it will mean that those who don't will gain the advantage.

Governments look with greedy eyes on the land and resources of other nations while those who seek to intervene in the resultant clashes are often guilty of operating not for the well-being of the combatants, but in their own "best interest." Greed has led to war, to murder, to envy, to hatred, to theft, to adultery and to every other sin known to man. It is, therefore, not surprising to find that the Lord gave the clear commandment, "Thou shalt not covet" in the list of instructions whereby the people He had made should order their lives.

It is interesting to note that at least three different words were used in the Greek New Testament to describe "greed" and each word gives a slightly different insight. *Epithumeo* speaks of greed as being a passionate desire. *Pleonexia* means, literally, "to have more," and *philarguria* means "the love of silver." Many of us are painfully aware of the passion with which we devote ourselves to our own profit, and the zeal with which we pursue our own ends. It is a well-known fact that in some Communist countries where the workers have been given tracts of land to produce crops for the state, and alongside they have cultivated their own tract, that their own land has produced much more than the state's land!

"The love of money" is, as we all know, "the root

of all evil" and even though the quotation has been misquoted consistently there is no problem for people to recognize that when it comes to lining our pockets many other considerations go by the board. Recently, Johnny Carson was reading letters children had written to Santa Claus and he pointed out to his nationwide audience that the kids who came from "good" homes had lists of requests as long as their arms, but the kids from poor homes asked for much less and usually wanted the things they requested to go to someone other than themselves! Greed always wants more!

Self-Gratification in Place of God

Scripture is particularly scathing about greed stating that it stems from an evil heart along with "evil thoughts, sexual immorality, theft, murder . . ." and many other readily recognizable sins (see Mark 7:21,22). It adds in Romans 1:28 that greed is the result of a "depraved mind." And Ephesians 4:19 states that greed can be traced back to people "having lost all sensitivity" because of their rejection of God. Perhaps the most damning statement about greed is to be found in Colossians 3:5 where we are told that greed is "idolatry."

Careful consideration of these things will show that the greed that brings war and hate, murder and inequity to our world is not going to be cured through well-meaning programs or well-financed schemes although these things may, and indeed should, alleviate some of the consequences of greed. The real problem is a heart problem which is related to man's rejection of God and man's installation of self-gratification in the place of God.

The rich man, as he spoke to himself about his plans, sprinkled his sentences liberally with his favorite words, "I, my, myself" showing quite clearly that he was first and foremost an egotist. His preoccupation with his "goods" even to the point of total disregard of eternal and spiritual considerations showed him to be a rank materialist and his classic statement, "Take life easy; eat, drink and be merry" which wrapped up his whole philosophy of life is still the watchword of hedonists worldwide.

There is no doubt that the farmer derived considerable enjoyment from his materialism as he heaped up his measurable tokens of success. As he did so his "friends" were only too delighted to help him spend his money and enjoy the products of his labor. This served to boost his ego and further his egotistical bent. As everyone who has ever sat down to a good meal with good friends can testify, there is a lot to be said for eating, drinking and being merry.

So there is no point disputing the fact that the rich man lived the "good life" and thoroughly enjoyed it. Equally there is no point denying that the good life had led him to such a selfish, greedy, earthbound existence that he became a totally withered person, shortly due to leave his world and his life, and be confronted with the world he had ignored and the life to which he was dead.

Jesus could sense this awful possibility in the lives of the two brothers—the one who was complaining about not getting his share and the one who had cheated his own brother. In the Master's eyes the squabble over "fair shares" was nowhere near as important as the presence of greed in both their lives and the consequences for them if nothing was done about it. His warning therefore, "Watch out! Be on your guard against all kinds of greed" was timely for them and necessary for all who have read the parable since it was taught.

Watch Out

How do we "Watch out"? How do we go about being on our "Guard against all kinds of greed"?

First we should *be aware of the powerful influence that material things exercise on our lives.* We like to be comfortable, happy, and well-cared-for and if we can provide for ourselves in these areas then we will probably find it is easy to become very busy in the provision for and satisfaction of our own needs. Soon, however, we become confused about the difference between a "need" and a "want" and if we are not careful we may become caught up in the provision for our own wants. While we are busy providing for wants we may well be neglecting the needs of others and our concentration of this task may get our attention so focused on ourselves that we will not only lose sight of the needy around us but also begin to ignore the realities of the spiritual and the eternal world.

Secondly, we should be aware of the fact that because we live in a secularized world, governed by secular considerations and operated on secular motivations, *we cannot help but be influenced by the secularism all round us.* The pressure of maintaining the status quo, the continual bombardment of materialistic advertising and popular philosophies of the age and the nation all have their impact upon us which, if not countered, will make us more greedy and less sacrificial, more earth-bound and less heaven-minded. The way to counter these pressures is to continually expose yourself to the Word of God so that you might be aware of the real world of eternity and in touch with the real values of the Eternal.

Thirdly, we should never forget that *it is perfectly natural to be greedy!* If we do overlook this fact we may slide into a life of self-centeredness and not even be able to recognize it. See yourself as a basically

71

egotistical, materialistic individual and be on your guard for every evidence of it.

When you see yourself functioning in this way take steps to say no to yourself and yes to the Holy Spirit, yielding yourself to what He has been saying to you in the Word of God, obeying Him rather than your own desires, following His dictates rather than your own inclinations. This will require a considerable degree of personal insight, spiritual discernment and disciplined behavior in the power of the Spirit of God. But bear in mind the admonition to "Watch out" and remember the words of the Master, "This is how it will be with anyone who stores up things for himself and is not rich toward God." This should be adequate motivation to move in the right direction.

Finally, *inventory your own possessions.* Take some time out to go through your checkbook and see what proportion of your earnings went on yourself and how much was devoted to the concerns and needs of others. Check on the way you spend your time and see how much of it is invested in yourself and how much is channeled into the work of the Lord. Look at your will and see how you have been approaching the future and what things are really important enough to you to be remembered in the disposition of your estate. Then sit down with the Lord and work on your budget and say to Him, "Lord, all I have is thine and I have a terrible tendency to regard it as mine. All I am is yours but I have an inbuilt capacity to regard my life as mine. I keep to myself what I wish, and do with my life as I desire and I recognize this to be basically selfish and greedy. Thank you for warning about the end results of greed and please show me how to budget my time, resources and life so that all will be invested for you and Eternity in terms of my life among people on earth."

6 Readiness—The Watchword for the Faithful

Luke 12:35-48—The Wedding Feast

"Be dressed ready for service and keep your lamps burning, like men waiting for their master to return from a wedding banquet, so that when he comes and knocks they can immediately open the door for him. It will be good for those servants whose master finds them watching when he comes. I tell you the truth, he will dress himself to serve, will have them recline at the table and will come and wait on them. It will be good for those servants whose master finds them ready, even if he comes in the second or third watch of the night. But understand this: If the owner of the house had known at what hour the thief was coming, he would not have let his house be broken into. You also must be ready, because the Son of Man will come at an hour when you do not expect him."

Peter asked, "Lord, are you telling this parable to us, or to everyone?"

The Lord answered, "Who then is the faithful and wise manager, whom the master puts in charge of his servants to give them their food allowance at the proper time? It will be good for that servant whom the master finds doing so when he returns. I tell you the truth, he will put him in charge of all his possessions. But suppose the servant says to himself, 'My master is taking a long time in coming,' and he then begins to beat the menservants and womenservants and to eat and drink and get drunk. The master of that servant will come on a day when he does not expect him and at an hour he is not aware of. He will cut him to pieces and assign him a place with the unbelievers.

"That servant who knows his master's will and does not get ready or does not do what his master wants will be beaten with many blows. But the one who does not know and does things deserving punishment will be beaten with few blows. From everyone who has been given much, much will be demanded; and from the one who has been entrusted with much, much more will be asked.

Some time ago one of my close Christian friends discovered that she had cancer. After much prayer, counsel and medical treatment we decided to hold a special gathering of believing friends to pray together that the Lord might see fit to bring about healing. About a dozen of us came together and I asked the lady concerned if she would share with us what had transpired in her life since she discovered her illness. She gladly responded to the invitation and gave a detailed testimony to God's faithfulness, the comfort of the Scriptures, the support of the believing community and the enrichment in her own personal and family life. Her husband, when she had concluded, said with great difficulty and much emotion, "It's been a great experience."

I was interested to hear more from him as to why he should regard this event as a great experience when most people would see it as a tragic intrusion. Before he could answer one of the ladies in the group said, "Oh, I know what he means. I had cancer 16 years ago and through it all I was brought to realize how shallow my life was."

She had scarcely finished speaking before another person said, "I had extremely serious surgery years ago and was hospitalized for three months, hanging on to life by a thread. But through that experience I learned some things I would never have learned in any other way."

His wife waited till he had finished and added, "It was awful seeing him suffer but we grew so much as persons and as a family through the whole terrible time."

As one person after another spoke I looked at the faces of the people in the room. The pretty blonde whose husband deserted her and their two young sons, the widow whose pastor husband died a slow death ministering all the time to those who were ill all around him, the businessman and his wife whose son had been killed in a train accident just 12 months previously. They were all close to tears but they were all nodding their heads in agreement and with understanding. They were all convinced that they had learned things through adversity that they had not been ready to learn before tragedy came their way.

Immersed in Life

We talked a long time and came to the conclusion that life is so full of exciting, interesting, challenging, frightening things and people that we can very easily become so immersed in life that we forget to stop and think carefully about where our lives are heading. But the incidence of illness and death quickly changes all that.

The husband of the wife with cancer said, "Fellowship which I always believed in is so precious to me now. My family which was so important is so much more important now. My Bible which I have read for years speaks to me so clearly now, and the Lord whom I have known for years is more real to me than ever before."

The lady whose son had been killed, said quietly, "The questions that used to be so big and so important are now so unimportant. All that matters now is that we know He is Lord."

The man who had been ill in the hospital for months added, "The way I learned in the hospital to look at the little I had left has affected the way I've looked at everything else ever since."

Although I had known all this before, I was once again reminded how unfortunate it is that we human beings seem to be so preoccupied with secondary things in this life that it takes an intervention of monumental proportions to get us to the place where we will even begin to think about the things that really matter.

Winston Churchill, in the early thirties, tried with all his considerable powers to awaken the English-speaking world to the impending dangers of a resurgent Germany under "Corporal Hitler" but to no avail. It was ironic that he should be asked to lead Britain in her fight against Nazism after he had done so much to try to avert the war. This sense of irony never left him as is clearly evident in the fact that when Roosevelt asked him what he felt the war should be called he answered without hesitation, "The Unnecessary War." Churchill of all people knew how hard it is to get people to listen to what they don't want to hear and be confronted with that which may affect their life-styles. Only calamity will make them take notice of those things which they should be noticing all the time.

Note of Urgency

There was a note of urgency about the ministry of Jesus as He taught the crowds in general and His disciples in particular. As we saw in the previous chapter, His warning about greed as illustrated by the story of "the man who had everything" but was in danger of finding he possessed nothing, was necessary because the peoples' orientation was not towards spiritual realities. He followed that story with a similar parable designed to alert His hearers to the importance of realizing that the life they were living was not open-ended. They, like most people who have ever lived, were assuming a kind of immortality and giving little or no thought to the brevity of life and the uncertainty of existence.

However, the Master introduced a new concept in the parable about the wedding banquet. His stimulus to thinking about eternal rather than temporal matters was not death or illness but the fact that "the Son of Man will come at an hour when you do not expect him." The response expected from such a statement was that His disciples must be "ready." In other words, while we recognize the immense value of illness and adversity as stimuli to serious thought and reassessment of values, an understanding of the doctrine of the "return of Christ" should have the same effect without our going through the anguish of traumatic experiences. It ought to be possible for believers to be serious about their commitment to Christ even though they may not have gone through earth-shaking experiences or been confronted with potentially life-shattering problems.

"While the cat's away, the mice will play" is a principle of human as well as rodent behavior! Jesus didn't exactly use this expression but He showed familiarity with the concept when He related the story of the man who went off to a wedding. His household was left in the hands of his numerous servants who were given responsibility for the maintenance and well-being of the property. There was, of course, a great temptation for them to do a minimum of work so that all would appear to have been cared for and to spend the surplus time drinking the master's wine and smoking his cigars. Responsible servants would resist this temptation and knowing how to conduct themselves in a more mature manner would be active in fulfilling their master's wishes as well as eagerly awaiting his return.

Ready for the Master

In the special circumstances in which servants in the East worked in Christ's day, they would be careful to hitch their long flowing robes into their belts to give them greater freedom for manual labor, they would carefully tend the wicks of the lamps and replenish the oil so that the lamps would burn brightly, and their ears would be wide open to hear the sound of the master's arrival.

Rather surprisingly, Jesus said that those servants who behaved in such an exemplary fashion would be given the privilege of having the master tell them to sit down and he would serve them!

This kind of thing happens once a year at Christmas time in the Royal Navy, when the officers serve the "men" much to the delight of all those who normally have to do the serving! Perhaps, the Lord was giving a somewhat humorous illustration at this point to bring home to His hearers the benefits accruing to those who work with a sense of responsibility and fulfill their commitments with thoroughness. While we cannot be sure of the tone of voice when He said these words or the facial expression which might have given us a clue to His meaning, there is no doubt about the point He was making! "It will be good for those servants whose master finds them ready" was His summary of the situation. Then turning to His hearers He made the powerful statement, "You also must be ready."

Peter who was famous for a number of things was also the unanimous choice of the disciples for the title, "the disciple most likely to ask questions." "Lord, are you telling this parable to us, or to everyone?" he asked. Maybe he was a little worried about the force of the Master's words, particularly if they were being directed exclusively to the little group of disciples, and he felt that the demands would not be quite so great if they were spread over a wider area.

We will never know what Peter had in mind when he asked his question, but it is interesting to note that Jesus didn't get around to answering it in unequivocal terms. As we know, the Master had a habit of answering some questions by asking a question in return. On other occasions He simply refused to answer, but this time He just kept talking! "Good servants who handle their responsibilities well, get promoted. But those who get tired of waiting and decide that their load is too heavy or their responsibility too onerous sometimes get irritated and negligent and may even start taking their frustrations out on the people left in their charge. Those kind of people are heading for

79

trouble and if they are not careful, they stand to lose everything they hold dear."

Many believers today experience great difficulty understanding the doctrine of the "return of Christ" correctly. There are those who are so enamored of the subject that they appear to live their lives straining their necks towards the eastern skies, while others are so oblivious to the doctrine that they don't know which way is east!

Imagine the problem confronting the people to whom the Master spoke this parable. He was amongst them establishing the fact that He is the Son of Man. Many of His hearers were not at all sure what that meant and even His most ardent disciples were limited in their understanding of His ministry and mission, as is obvious from their behavior at the time of His death and their reactions to His resurrection. If they could not grasp His presence among them, they certainly had problems understanding His departure from them. And it is clear that if they could not understand His departure then His return must have been almost totally incomprehensible. Nevertheless, the Master spoke of His return and apparently expected them to grasp something of its significance. And He certainly expected them to live in the light of its certainty.

Certainty and Uncertainty

We have a decided advantage over those who were present when this parable was taught because, with the benefit of the knowledge the Spirit has given to us, we can see much more clearly than Christ's contemporaries the whole plan of the Father outlined in the Incarnation, Crucifixion, Resurrection, Ascension and Return. This knowledge is intended to produce an air of calm certainty that, whatever else may or may not happen in this world, Christ will come in great power and glory to establish His eternal Kingdom.

The certainty of this return is, however, mingled with a delightful touch of uncertainty. For while believers know He will come, they do not know when He will come. It is the correct mixture of certainty and uncertainty that produces the right response of calm assurance and eager anticipation. To know exactly when He is coming would probably produce in some disciples, the attitude of college students who know they have six months to finals! But even that kind of attitude is to be preferred to the attitude of many students when they know there won't be any finals! The ideal situation, if you want to keep both believers and students on their toes (and their knees!), is to let them know there will be finals but not to let them know exactly when the finals will be held; although sufficient signs should be given to let both know that something "is in the wind."

Signs of the Times

Care should be taken in the interpretation of the "signs of the times." It is easy either to ignore them completely or to become so obsessed by them that everything that happens in the world can be interpreted as an indication of the immediate return of Christ. If we bear in mind the Master's clear word, "No one knows about that day or hour, not even the angels in heaven, nor the Son, but only the Father" (Matt. 24:36), we will avoid falling into the trap dug by those who endeavor to work out what even the angels and the Son didn't know. But at the same time, we must not ignore the clear indications that show His coming is drawing nearer every day. Perhaps our attitude to the signs of the times should be that we

81

recognize they are not designed to state the date, but to prepare the state of mind. A state of mind characterized by eagerness and preparedness.

Attitudes play such an important part in all activities. Careless people seldom produce effectively, lazy people never work to potential, and the unmotivated waste their time and their talents. But how to motivate people is, and always has been, a problem. This was certainly the case of the people in the parable, and, without doubt, it is true of many who are the disciples of Christ.

I am convinced that a true sense of privilege is one of the greatest possible motivating factors. The words used in the parable are interesting: "servants," "owner," "manager," and "master." Some people react to such words, particularly if they feel that they are the ones being owned, managed, mastered or required to serve. But a little thought will show that no man is an island; therefore, everybody has to be on the receiving end of this kind of relationship at some point in his life; therefore, there is nothing intrinsically bad about the experience. In fact, the value of being in such a relationship is determined by a consideration of the owner and master and his attitude to his servants. If he is a worthy man, widely trusted and universally respected, then to be related to him is an honor. If he is known to be the sort of person who will sit servants down at table and make a meal for them occasionally it would be reasonable to assume that potential servants would be standing in line waiting for the old servants to die off and the stupid ones to be fired.

The Son of Man obviously regarded His status as the Servant of Jehovah with great joy and His commission to "do His will" as a delight. To acknowledge Christ as Lord is similarly joyful and to be known as

His servant is to be warmed by a sense of great privilege.

Trustworthy Because He Trusted Them

The master of the parable was a man who expected his servants to be trustworthy because he trusted them. To require responsibility of a person who is not given responsibility is nonsense. This sense of being trusted and made responsible can be greatly encouraging. Servants of Christ should constantly recognize that they are not mindless instruments or programmed machines plugged into God's monolithic plan. They, like the servants of the parable, are not dishwashing machines that can only wash dishes when switched on, or vacuum cleaners that can only vacuum when plugged in. They are people with the capacity to know and love the Master and with the capability to know what to do in order to express their love and devotion. They have been trusted and they are responsible.

Some servants do not respond either to a sense of privilege or responsibility. To them it matters not that their master thinks highly enough of them to trust them and they are unmoved by the thought that they are not acting in a mature manner when they take their money without doing their job. Their attitude is "a fair day's pay for a fair day's shirk."

It is a well-known fact that even such reprehensible characters have been known to respond to another kind of stimulus. Jesus expressed Himself with frightening intensity when He explained that anyone who falls into the category just described will discover his master will "cut him to pieces and assign him a place with the unbelievers." Whatever else He meant by this, the Master certainly intended to convey the fact that such a thing as punishment exists for those who are unfaithful in the same way that those who are faithful and eager to serve will reap the benefits of being served by their master. The promise of reward and the threat of punishment may well motivate those servants not motivated by more noble considerations.

The Lord, when talking about this aspect of service, explained that punishment and reward will be graduated. Those servants who knew very little about their service and the Master's requirements will naturally not be held as responsible as those who were fully acquainted with the details of their service. In the same way, those who have been given great opportunity and superior ability will be expected to produce more for the glory of God and the well-being of the society in which they were placed and to which they were sent. The solemn words of Christ ought to be etched deeply on the conscience of every believer in the parts of the world where great opportunity to learn and to grow, to work and to share has been made available. "From everyone who has been given much, much will be demanded; and from the one who has been entrusted with much, much more will be asked."

Between the Lines

Peter, as we saw, did not get a direct answer to his question as to whether the Lord was talking about the small group of disciples or everyone in general, but I'm sure that he had no difficulty reading between the lines and coming up with the answer that he perhaps didn't want! He and his friends had been given much, and so they were expected to do, with great success, that which they had been given to do. They had been entrusted with monumental responsibility so they were expected to achieve great things in the power of

God. That they were remarkably successful in their ministry of making Christ known is evident from the fact that 2,000 years after their decease we are reading their works, writing books about what they said and being given the opportunity of following on where they left off.

But don't forget that while we didn't see the Master face to face as they did, we certainly have a greater revelation of the truth given to us in the completed Word of God. Also, the means of doing the work to which we have been called are so much more sophisticated than anything they could even have imagined. In fact, the opportunities given to the church of Christ in this age are equalled only by the need that surrounds us. So we should make sure, as never before, that we are servants who work diligently and effectively because of our highly developed sense of privilege, our deep sense of obligation, our eager anticipation of the Lord's return, and the thought of the ultimate evaluation which He will place on our work.

7 Fruitfulness— Evidence of Repentance

Luke 13:1-9—The Barren Fig Tree

Now there were some present at that time who told Jesus about the Galileans whose blood Pilate had mixed with their sacrifices. Jesus answered, "Do you think that these Galileans were worse sinners than all the other Galileans because they suffered this way? I tell you, no! But unless you repent, you too will all perish. Or those eighteen who died when the tower in Siloam fell on them—do you think they were more guilty than all the others living in Jerusalem? I tell you, no! But unless you repent, you too will all perish."

Then he told this parable: "A man had a fig tree, planted in his vineyard, and he went to look for fruit on it, but did not find any. So he said to the man who took care of the vineyard, 'For three years now I've been coming to look for fruit on this fig tree and haven't found any. Cut it down! Why should it use up the soil?'

" 'Sir,' the man replied, 'leave it alone for one more year, and I'll dig around it and fertilize it. If it bears fruit next year, fine! If not, then cut it down.' "

It has been said that when churches are looking for a pastor they sometimes search for a man who will be totally fearless and uncompromising as he tells them exactly what they want to hear! Sad to say, there is more than an element of truth in this statement because church people, like most people, much prefer flattery to challenge and find encouragement much easier to take than correction.

A few months ago I met a fine young man in South Africa who told me that he had decided to quit the pastoral ministry. I was most concerned to hear this and when I asked him why he had arrived at such a major decision he said he just couldn't get anywhere with the people to whom he was trying to minister. Because of their particular cultural and political orientation they were not prepared to accept some of the things that he was teaching them from Scripture and so he had decided that he was wasting his time.

I advised him to give a little more thought to his position before resigning, but encouraged him to continue in his exposition of Scripture, to maintain an attitude of loving concern for the people and to be patient in his dealings with them in their struggles to apply scriptural principles to deep-rooted tradition. He was more than a little skeptical about his chances of success and questioned me about whether I had any idea what he was going through. I assured him that I did have some experience in this area, but more importantly I reminded him that Ezekiel and Jere-

87

miah, Peter and Paul, Bunyan and Niemöller and countless other saints had gone through similar situations. That helped! But it was not until I reminded him of the ministry of Christ to His contemporaries and the reactions that He faced that he was able to say, "Okay, I'll go and preach the Word to them and wait on God to bring about a change of heart until it becomes apparent that they are irrevocably resisting the Spirit."

Fire upon the Earth

The Master Himself certainly did not tell the people what they wanted to hear and it is no surprise, therefore, that He did not always get the response from them that He desired. He said quite firmly that He had not come to bring peace, but a sword and as a result of His teachings even families would be split. He characterized His ministry as bringing "fire on the earth" (Luke 12:49). There is, of course, a real sense in which Christ did bring peace to troubled hearts and rest to weary souls, but this aspect of His ministry should never be emphasized to the detriment of the balancing aspect that even the message of peace will produce division. For every person who gets excited about Christ and responds positively, there will always be one who reacts in the opposite way and if the new believer has any close contact with such a person the sparks will probably fly.

This became very clear when the Master began to speak clearly and forcibly to the religious people of His day. He had an unsettling habit of calling people "hypocrites" and while there were those who agreed with His evaluation, there were many who took exception to what He said about them. I can easily imagine the kind of mealtime conversation in many a home after the family had heard Christ speak.

"Well, Dad, what did you think of the sermon today?"

"I was insulted!"

"Why? What did He say that upset you?"

"He said that if I was interested in weather forecasting that proved I was a hypocrite."

"Oh come off it, Dad, He didn't say anything of the sort. What He actually said was that if you take the time to become an expert in reading the skies so that you can predict the weather but won't take time to become an expert in spiritual matters when you profess to be spiritual then you are being inconsistent!"

"Well, I don't think He has any right to judge people like that and I certainly won't be going back to listen to Him again. In fact, I'm going to see if something can't be done to get Him silenced. We don't need that kind of talk around here."

"Well, Dad, I for one don't want Him silenced because what He said made a lot more sense than anything I've ever heard before. What He said about people in general fitted me personally like a second skin. Dad, I claim to be a God-fearer, but I'm more interested in secular things than spiritual. I make loud noises about the Lord but I wonder about the reality of my commitment to Him. I think He was absolutely right when He called me a hypocrite and even though the truth hurts, I'm going to accept it from Him and act upon what He says."

"That's your privilege but it's my privilege to let you know that if you're going to get into this kind of thing you and your pretty little wife can find somewhere else to live because I don't want you coming home each day giving me another load of His teachings."

"Wait a minute, this son of yours who you are ordering out of the house happens to be my son, too, and while I don't buy what Jesus was saying either, I think I ought to be consulted before my boy is made homeless."

"Thanks, Mom, I needed that!"

"Don't get any big ideas young man, I'm not saying that I agree with you or the Teacher because I don't. I wasn't upset about the weather watching because I'm not even sure what He was talking about, but I was upset to hear that Jesus has been teaching people to disobey the law of Moses. That's blasphemy."

"That's a new one on me. What are you talking about?"

"My friend told me that she heard Him say that people who observe the Sabbath are hypocrites."

"Oh, now I know what you mean! What He actually said was quite different from what you were told. A lady who had been ill for 18 years came to Him on the Sabbath and He healed her. The Pharisees who saw what He had done to her got out their little books, checked their lists and ruled that touching someone and healing them was work and as He had done it on the Sabbath He was breaking the law of Moses. To which He gave the classic answer, 'You hypocrites! Doesn't each of you on the Sabbath untie his ox or donkey from the stall and lead it out to give it water? Then should not this woman, a daughter of Abraham, whom Satan has kept bound for 18 years be set free on the Sabbath day from what bound her?' Mom, you should have seen their red faces because they knew He had exposed their hypocrisy."

Fantasy as Opposed to Reality

So it was when Christ preached. Arguments raged, tempers got frayed, families were divided against each other, "three against two, and two against three" (Luke 12:52). And much of the friction and conflict could be traced to His persistent use of the term "hypocrite." I think that people living in the Western world have a particular sensitivity to the word and feel extremely uneasy about the way and the regularity with which Christ used it. But we should remember that it means basically to act or project a fantasy as opposed to reality. Christ, who claimed to be the "Truth" (another word for reality), had to be opposed to anything that substituted fantasy for reality because He, more than anyone else, knew the mortal danger of living in self-induced fantasy instead of God-provided reality. To Him it was more important that people should confront reality than have their feelings hurt. He would much prefer a person to enter heaven with a bruised ego than enter hell with ego intact!

In the case of the weather forecasting hypocrites He saw people who were making great professions of spiritual insight whose sole insight was in the area of cloud formation. This He could not and would not allow to go unchallenged. Those who objected to Him healing on the Sabbath day were proud to be protectors of God's honor and guardians of His glory. But, in fact, they were only prepared to have God honored their way and the glory of God was only legitimate if it fitted their preconceived ideas and meshed with their own meticulously formulated formulas. So in reality, their commitment to honoring God was as much a figment of their own fantasy lives as the professed spiritual insights of their cloud-watching brethren.

Self-Satisfaction and Self-Righteousness

There was an all pervading sense of smugness, self-satisfaction and self-righteousness in the religious community of Christ's generation. This surfaced when Christ's hearers reminded Him of two tragedies that had happened in their recent history.

Pontius Pilate who had worked hard to become totally despised by the Jews had added to his notoriety by having some Galileans executed while they were in the act of worshiping. Their blood had been mingled with the blood of sacrifice, an unthinkable thing to all people and totally beyond the comprehension of the Jewish community. It was common in those days for such tragedies to be interpreted as God's way of bringing judgment upon the people who suffered. The people mentioned this because they assumed that the Galileans must have been particularly obnoxious sinners to have warranted such divine retribution, but as they themselves had not been judged in similar fashion, they were justified in regarding their status before God as perfectly satisfactory, irrespective of what Christ said.

They bolstered their argument by adding the story of the unfortunate people whose lives had been snuffed out without warning when a tower in Siloam collapsed on top of them. They were convinced that the people killed in the tower accident deserved it but they themselves were blameless, otherwise something equally terrible would have happened to them!

Jesus flatly rejected this reasoning and told the people that if they thought that the people killed in the Temple and under the tower were any more or less sinful, they were grossly mistaken. And if they assumed that these incidents proved their own innocence they were even more mistaken. In fact, if they didn't repent they would perish as surely as the accident victims.

The Caricature of Repentance

The term "repentance" requires a little explanation

for the same reason that "hypocrite" needs to be more clearly defined. We don't always understand what it means! There is a certain caricature about repentance that has led people to think that repentance is an emotional experience enjoyed by strange people who like to cry in public. These people are aided and abetted by men well-trained in the art of helping their fellowmen make fools of themselves. At certain times of the year and in certain well organized meetings people are encouraged to attend with a view to weeping and wailing their way to God, knowing full well that they will probably be back next year repenting some more. Caricature is the correct word for such an interpretation of the solemn word repentance.

Little better than this caricature is the approach that has identified repentance with penance and a ritual almost totally devoid of meaning. The attendance at obligatory "confession," the attempt to think of "something to tell him" and the apparently mechanical imposition of certain well-ordered exercises as a means of "doing penance," has led to a cheap degrading of "repentance."

To repent is literally to change the mind, but even this definition is inadequate in terms of our contemporary attitude to changes of mind. Today, to change the mind is synonymous to being uncommitted, undecided or both. We change our minds at the drop of a hat and when the next hat drops we change our minds about changing our minds. This leads to a trivializing of decision and a prostitution of commitment.

To change the mind in the biblical sense of repentance is, however, much more. It means to come to a conclusion that something is wrong when you previously had no thought that it was wrong; then to

93

decide to reject the wrong and take steps to avoid it in future and do the opposite—the right.

Repentance, therefore, is not necessarily emotional although it may, of course, be accompanied by tears. It is primarily intellectual and volitional, leading to a change of mind which produces changed attitudes demonstrated by changed actions. This is the repentance Christ demanded from His contemporaries which they were not all prepared to give.

The reality of repentance in terms of new attitude and new activity was clearly illustrated by the parable that the Master told after warning His hearers, "But unless you repent, you too will all perish."

Figless Fig Tree

A certain man who had planted a vineyard and taken exceptional care of it had also planted a fig tree in the vineyard. This was not an uncommon practice. For three years, the man watched his fig tree grow and become firmly established in the well nourished soil of the carefully tended vineyard. But unfortunately the fig tree failed to reproduce. This irritated the man because he wanted figs, felt that he had done all that could reasonably be expected of him to produce the figs and wasn't prepared to be denied his figs. In addition, he hated to waste his precious land. So he gave instructions to his vinedresser to rip out the guilty fig tree and put something in its place that would produce. The vinedresser was prepared to be a little more patient with the fig tree and suggested that it should be left for another year, given special treatment and then if it still didn't deliver the goods it should be removed. This was agreed upon. Like all the parables the story line is simple in the extreme but the point being made is wonderfully profound.

As we have seen, there are innumerable people

whose lives are not being lived in the light of reality. Having been alerted to this fact, they need to repent. The essence of this repentance will be a changed life that will place a realistic approach where once fantasy reigned supreme. The repentant life is a life of openness to the claims of Christ where once there was avoidance and evasion often under the smoke screen of religion and piety. But when repentance is real, the fruit of repentance is evident. The inescapable thrust of the fig tree story is, therefore, a statement that unless there is tangible fruit or evidence of a revolutionary change there is no real repentance and where there is not real repentance there is only judgment. Pious, self-righteous Jews needed to hear this in case their cultural approach to religion should lead them unrepentantly to lostness. People in our world of today who attend church but assume that they are doing great must be alerted to their fantasies, led to repentance, and taught to evaluate their lives for evidences of the changed mind. Others, whose life-style is built on the precarious basis that just so long as they are sincere they will see everything turn out alright in the end, need to learn that they are really deluding themselves and must come to repentance towards God.

The Fruit Is Obedience

The fruit that is evidence is, of course, the life of obedience to the divine requirements. Prior to repentance the unrepentant person lives either in blatant, unrelenting disobedience or self-induced ignorance of the divine dictates. But once repentance has become part of the life, obedience becomes the stuff of which the new life is made. This requires a working knowledge of the things that God requires people to do and also an experience of the power to do what is required through the person of the Holy Spirit. "Fruit" is, therefore, the product of obedience to the known will of God and dependence upon the gracious working of the Spirit of God. Without this fruit there is no real repentance and that means there is no real salvation.

The patience of the vinedresser and the care with which he tended the unproductive fig tree is intended to convey the wonderful news that although the Lord will not tolerate unreality and will go on insisting on repentance, He is nevertheless remarkably longsuffering. The long history of God's dealings with His people, Israel, is a continuing story of divine forbearance, and even before the special relationship with the children of Abraham was established, God showed His patience in holding back judgment in the days of Noah while the Ark was being built and the ancient boat builder preached righteousness to his contemporaries.

Patience and Forbearance of God

Fig trees, so far as we know, do not have the ability to recognize patience on the part of their owners so it is not surprising that they are not moved by such benevolence expressed to them. Humans, however, can recognize patience and are capable of being aware of the divine longsuffering. It is, therefore, deeply disappointing that men often use the forbearance of God as an argument against the certainty of judgment instead of gratefully acknowledging the divine grace and responding positively.

In much the same way, fig trees can't recognize the ongoing opportunity that is theirs by reason of the ground space alloted to them. Neither can they possibly recognize the cost of the fertilizer placed around their roots. But humans who want to know can always discover the privilege that is theirs and the expensive care that is lavished upon them. Understanding these things should lead to rapid repentance rather than to casual exploitation of the blessings of opportunity and nurture for selfish ends.

Never reject the possibility that your life is more related to fantasy than reality when it comes to spiritual issues and when you come to this point never allow the patience and ongoing goodness of God to postpone necessary repentance. And remember that the Master is constantly looking for evidence that the change of mind concerning Him and His objectives for your life is being worked out in your experience.

8 Smallness— Potential for Power

Luke 13:18-21—Mustard Seed and Yeast

Then Jesus asked, "What is the kingdom of God like? What shall I compare it to? It is like a mustard seed, which a man took and planted in his garden. It grew, became a tree, and the birds of the air perched in its branches."

Again he asked, "What shall I compare the kingdom of God to? It is like yeast that a woman took and mixed into a large amount of flour until it worked all through the dough."

The Greenside Choir was short of tenors. That was the only reason the leader asked me to become a member! I was happy to accept the invitation because the choir was regarded in British musical circles as one of the best in the nation. On one memorable occasion we were granted the opportunity to sing at the National Eisteddfod in North Wales. We decided to compete recognizing that even though we would be singing against some of the best choirs in Britain we were one of the favorites to win the coveted prize.

We didn't win. But it was not so much our defeat that surprised us as the way in which we were defeated. A choir from Italy was entered in the competition but nobody attached any importance to them because they were unknown and embarrassingly small. In fact, their choir was strictly an octet! So nobody gave them a chance of succeeding in competition which for years had been dominated by choirs numbering anything up to 200 voices. When they started to sing everybody realized those eight voices were producing choral sounds the like of which had never been heard at the National Eisteddfod before or since. They were superb and absolutely nobody objected when they won the competition. The other choirs had discounted them because they had fallen for the old misconception that "bigger is better" which as we ought to know, is as erroneous a concept as "might is right."

The Potential of Small Things

Besides tending to be confused about the relative worth of small things in a world that worships at the shrine of greatness, we also have a tendency to overlook the potential of the small or the hidden things. A few days ago I was privileged to watch a surgeon friend perform an emergency operation. The patient was critically ill and it was obvious from X-rays and examinations that there was some kind of perforation in his abdomen. When the abdomen was opened it took only a few seconds to locate the problem which was a perforated duodenal ulcer. I was amazed that such a tiny hole could be responsible for such a critical condition. But small things can do big things!

The big impact of smallness is not always bad. Recent developments in computer science continue to boggle the imagination. For instance, IBM recently announced that they had developed a tiny electronic chip, no bigger than a diamond in a ring, that could hold 64,000 pieces of information. Only a few years ago it took a roomful of equipment to do the same thing!

The Mustard Seed and the Yeast

It was the greatness of smallness which was on the Master's mind when He told the parables of the mustard seed and the yeast. Pointing out to His listeners the tininess of the mustard seed He reminded them that such a tiny seed, when planted, grows in some instances to be 10 or 12 feet tall, big enough for birds to choose as their nesting place.

He followed this with a reminder that a little yeast put in a large amount of flour will very quickly affect the whole lump of dough. He used these illustrations to explain the strange workings of the Kingdom of God among men. Workings which do not necessarily operate on the basis of "bigger is better" or "might is right" but rather on the principle that small things have great value and produce big things in the experience and growth of the Kingdom.

It is interesting to realize that His statements concerning the Kingdom were prompted by the incident which we mentioned briefly in the last chapter when He healed the crippled woman on the Sabbath. He claimed that the woman's illness was directly related to the activity of Satan, stating with great authority, that she had been "kept bound" by Satan for 18 long years. He, therefore, believed in the invisible but powerful workings of Satan in people's lives, a working which can only be countered by an equally invisible but powerful working of the Kingdom of God. In fact, He clearly saw His ministry as a direct attack on the force of evil and its insidious hold on the lives of men.

As He moved among men He repeatedly endeavored to establish the Kingdom of God in the lives of those previously dominated by the activity of Satan.

I have noticed that people are prepared to talk about evil and even Satan when big, terrible things happen. When Jim Jones led his people down to the jungles of Guyana and encouraged them to build a paradise there which turned into a green hell on earth where 913 of the people perished, I was bombarded with questions about evil. At the risk of being misunderstood, however, I endeavored to point out that the activity of the force of evil in Jim Jones, and through him to the hundreds of unfortunates caught in his megalomaniacal trap, was different only in terms of numbers from the activities of evil that go on all around us day and night. But being the way we are, we tend to disregard the apparently insignificant until the spectacular comes along all the time failing to remember that the Master tried to tell us that the constant working of Satan in our world, as quietly and as invisible as the working of yeast in dough, is equally as powerful and dangerous as the evil witnessed in the camps of Guyana or Buchenwald.

The Quiet Working of Evil

The fact that Satan is blinding and binding people every minute they live is easily overlooked or ignored. This pleases the hellish genius immensely because, while he has innumerable problems in his own perverted personality, he has no hang-ups about being ignored so long as he can achieve his nefarious ends while being ignored.

Some dear friends of mine were invited to lead the music and teach the Word of God at a retreat center high in the San Bernardino mountains of California. Living in the Los Angeles basin with all its smog and attendant allergies they didn't need a second invitation. So with great joy they headed for the hills for what they expected would be an idyllic weekend. Little did they know that as a result of that weekend the young mother of three would, within a few days, lie at death's door surrounded by perplexed physicians who knew only that she was dying. Fortunately, an astute laboratory technician discovered evidence of a rare condition of the blood which had been caused by a tiny tick bite that had been overlooked. The bigness of smallness once again had almost been overlooked to the point of disaster, but fortunately her life was saved and she fully recovered.

It is particularly troublesome that the quiet working of evil is so often disregarded by those in whose lives the activity is taking place. We see from the Lord's statement that the woman's illness was related to Satan's "binding" activity. It is clear that he had been active in a "blinding" way too, otherwise they would have known it was his activity without the Lord having to tell them. Satan had, in effect, been as successful in blinding them as he had been successful in binding her.

To live and move blindly is to exist in hazardous fashion. To be blind to the possibility of blindness is even worse, but to be alerted to this reality is to be introduced to a spiritual concept of prime significance. It is my observation that the biblical teaching that "the god of this age has blinded the minds of unbelievers, so that they cannot see the light of the gospel of the glory of Christ" (2 Cor. 4:4) is to a large extent disbelieved even by professing believers—surely, the greatest imaginable proof of the accuracy of the statement.

Factor of Spiritual Blindness

How the blinding process takes place is possibly open to debate but there can be little doubt that false insights are gained one at a time slowly but surely without the person concerned even being aware of what is taking place. It ought to be a matter of concern, therefore, that the massive buildup of seemingly unrelated and apparently trivial items of information in our consciousness can be a major contributory factor to spiritual blindness. Add to this the possibility of subconscious assimilation of error masquerading as truth, and the stark reality of insidious control of thought and behavior becomes understandable. The Master said nothing about "brainwashing techniques" or "subliminal manipulation." He just talked about the blindness that comes from the quiet, unobtrusive working of evil in our lives.

The blindness of the people who witnessed the healing of the woman extended beyond their inability to see the spiritual aspects of her condition to their unwillingness to recognize the social extremities of her case. Their callous, insensitive indifference and marked lack of compassion, all in the name of God, were indicative of the remarkable success Satan has enjoyed in his ancient ways of working. Without fanfare or spectacle he has achieved his will in the lives of countless people as invisibly as yeast has its way with dough. The people in whom this activity is taking place are not only unaware of it but probably would deny it vehemently when presented with the evidence.

When Lemuel Gulliver arrived in Lilliput he knew he would have no problems with the six-inch-high Lilliputians but he realized how wrong he had been when he woke from sleep to discover he was immobilized by countless tiny threads fastened to countless tiny stakes secured by the tiny people. Not one stake, thread, or Lilliputian could have handled "Man Mountain," as he was known, but his blindness to the potential binding power of a quiet multiplication of these things led to his undoing.

Power of the Kingdom

It seems almost churlish to spend so much time thinking about the powerful impact of evil in our world and man's apparent inability or unwillingness to recognize and admit it. But it was clear that the Master insisted that people not only be alerted to the power of evil, but also that they should be cognizant of the counteracting power of the Kingdom of God which alone can deal with the situation. It was His demonstration of the power of the Kingdom overcoming the power of the Evil One which led to the parables we are considering. His point was unmistakably clear that if evil can start small and be so big so can the Kingdom, and if the influence of evil can spread quietly and quickly like yeast through dough, so also can the Kingdom.

The meaning of the Kingdom of God has been much debated among believers and it must be admitted that Scripture does present many and varied aspects of the Kingdom which understandably have led to a number of interpretations and emphases. However, these differences should never be allowed to divert our thinking from the basic, unarguable fact that whatever else Kingdom means it has to be related to the sphere of influence in which the King is recognized as such. By definition, therefore, the Kingdom of God must be that sphere of experience both human and cosmic, immediate and ultimate, present and future where God functions as King. Where this is the case, the power of God is released quietly, efficiently and in ever-increasing effectiveness.

When believers think of God we quite rightly think of His omnipotence, but then we sometimes make a mistake. Because we think of omnipotence as something that equips the one who possesses it to have his own way at all times, and because we know how we love the power to get our own way, we anticipate that God will use His power the way we would use it. A kind of "Hey there you, get out of my way. Don't you know who I am? I'm the all-powerful one and you'd better believe it because I'm going to get things done my way around here. If you don't like it you'd better just say so right now and be out of this place in 10 minutes flat." God prefers the mustard and yeast method.

The Mustard Seed and Yeast Method

When Elijah fled to Horeb rather than face the vicious and vindictive Jezebel, God asked him what he was doing and decided that Elijah needed a refresher course on "who God is." He was told, "Go out and stand on the mountain in the presence of the Lord, for the Lord is about to pass by" (1 Kings 17:11). He did so and was treated to a most remarkable spectacle. First "a great and powerful wind tore the mountains apart and shattered the rocks before the Lord." Shortly afterwards came an earthquake which was followed by a fire. None of this could possibly have caused Elijah any surprise because he knew his God was big. The surprise was that the Lord was not in the wind, the earthquake or the fire. He came in "a gentle whisper" which is just the way He likes to work so often! (See 1 Kings 19:11-13.)

When God decided to invade planet earth with Himself and give a fallen humanity a vision of His Being and an experience of His person he chose not to come in angelic form, in extra-terrestrial glory, or in unveiled, unmistakable divine majesty and blow everybody straight out of their tiny little minds. He chose a baby form, a poor nation, a humble stable and a servant role. Another example of the mustard method!

Later, after the Master had done His redemptive work and decided to delegate the ongoing work of building His church, He held no large rally, conducted no extensive seminar but rather committed the whole massive undertaking to a pitifully small band of disciples who had spent a large part of their training time misunderstanding Him and irritating each other. Yet knowing this He left them to it believing that through their insignificant contribution the whole world would hear the good news. He believed in the yeast method!

Perhaps the disciples, conscious as they must have been that they were not particularly impressive as potential world changers, took courage from their own history. Their nation, chosen by God to be the special means of blessing to the human race, started when God chose an unknown man who lived in Mesopotamia. The nation stumbled from tragedy to tragedy demonstrating little more than a penchant for disobedience and a fatal attraction to disaster. Yet it had survived despite its unpretentious beginnings and inauspicious behavior. And the disciples could do nothing but stand in awe of God's methods and shake their heads reverently saying with their favorite psalmist: "The Lord has done this, and it is marvelous in our eyes" (Ps. 118:23).

Divine Greatness

If it is true to say, as we have said, that contemporary man is in danger of forgetting the bigness of smallness in the activities of Satan, it is equally true to say that we have forgotten the parallel truth that there is divine greatness in many small things that God is doing. His method for establishing His Kingdom is to approach an individual, present him with the good news that he can be a part of the Kingdom and experience the unbelievable blessing of the kingly reign of Christ in his life. The individual thus alerted to the truth is then given the priceless opportunity of deciding whose Kingdom he wishes to be part of. On the basis of that choice individuals are either born into the Kingdom as quietly as mustard seeds are dropped on fertile soil or are allowed the privilege of choosing not to participate, in which case they are allowed quietly to steer their own lives to disintegration.

Once born into the Kingdom the quiet ministry of the Kingdom continues through the activity of the Indwelling King by His Spirit. The forces of evil are challenged by the power of the Spirit and as He is allowed His way in the believer's life, the unbinding and unblinding process picks up momentum. Few things excite me more than the opportunity to meet on a regular basis with new believers and help them recognize how their eyes are being opened to truth without their realizing it and that their lives are being liberated from bondage in ways they had not recognized.

Once individuals have begun to recognize the Kingdom strategy in their own lives it is not difficult for them to see how the strategy is intended to work on a broader base. For instance, new believers sometimes learn the hard way that their whole families are not going to convert to Christ simply because they "saw the light." After taking anything up to 25 years to acknowledge Christ themselves, for some strange reason, they expect the rest of the family to do it in 25 minutes. But this is not the way of the Kingdom. The believer in the unbelieving family should see himself as mustard, one small seed in a rather large field but working quietly and consistently towards the day when the whole family will be a tree. Families experiencing this kind of thing will then begin to discover their influence is not dissimilar to the influence of yeast. First attempts to start a neighborhood Bible study may meet with outright opposition or, what is worse, a promise to come which never materializes. But when the mustard and yeast method is recognized then the work of the Kingdom will continue.

In the same way, nations with great resources for Christ need to be continually thinking in terms of the planting of their mustard seeds in lands across the sea and nurturing the steady work of the Spirit through ministries which they support. They should not fall into the trap of expecting nations to turn to Christ overnight but they should anticipate the unrelenting work of the power of the King through their faithful commitment to His Kingdom until one day the answer to their constant prayer, "Your Kingdom come, your will be done" will materialize.

9 Selfishness— The Way to Down

Luke 14:1-24—The Great Banquet

One Sabbath, when Jesus went to eat in the house of a prominent Pharisee, he was being carefully watched. There in front of him was a man suffering from dropsy. Jesus asked the Pharisees and experts in the law, "Is it lawful to heal on the Sabbath or not?" But they remained silent. So taking hold of the man, he healed him and sent him away.

Then he asked them, "If one of you has a son or an ox that falls into a well on the Sabbath day, will you not immediately pull him out?" And they had nothing to say.

When he noticed how the guests picked the places of honor at the table, he told them this parable. "When someone invites you to a wedding feast, do not take the place of honor, for a person more distinguished than you may have been invited. If so, the host who invited both of you will come and say to you, 'Give this man your seat.' Then, humiliated, you will have to take the least important place. But when you are invited, take the lowest place, so that when your host comes, he will say to you, 'Friend, move up to a better place.' Then you will be honored in the presence of all your fellow guests. For everyone who exalts himself will be humbled, and he who humbles himself will be exalted."

Then Jesus said to his host, "When you give a luncheon or dinner, do not invite your friends, your brothers or relatives, or your rich neighbors; if you do, they may invite you back and so you will be repaid. But when you give a banquet, invite the poor, the crippled, the lame, the blind, and you will be blessed. Although they cannot repay you, you will be repaid at the resurrection of the righteous."

When one of those at the table with him heard this, he said to Jesus, "Blessed is the man who will eat at the feast in the kingdom of God." Jesus replied: "A certain man was preparing a great banquet and invited many guests. At the time of the banquet he sent his servant to tell those who had been invited, 'Come, for everything is now ready.'

"But they all alike began to make excuses. The first said, 'I have just bought a field, and I must go and see it. Please excuse me.'

"Another said, 'I have just bought five yoke of oxen, and I'm on my way to try them out. Please excuse me.'

"Still another said, 'I just got married, so I can't come.'

"The servant came back and reported this to his master. Then the owner of the house became angry and ordered his servant, 'Go out quickly into the streets and alleys of the town and bring in the poor, the crippled, the blind and the lame.'

" 'Sir,' the servant said, 'what you ordered has been done, but there is still room.'

"Then the master told his servant, 'Go out to the roads and country lanes and make them come in, so that my house will be full. I tell you, not one of those men who were invited will get a taste of my banquet.' "

Anyone who travels by air will have noticed a peculiar human characteristic: as soon as the airplane touches the ground, the cabin attendant reminds the passengers to check all their personal belongings and asks them to remain seated until the aircraft arrives at the gate and the seat belt sign is turned off. This announcement is the signal for some people to leap to their feet, scramble for their coats in the overhead racks and head down the aisle stumbling and swaying with the uneven momentum of the plane. Usually the announcement is repeated which gives people another chance to ignore it and place themselves and other passengers in some degree of jeopardy from falling baggage and bodies.

I have often observed that if people behave like this when all is well, what would it be like to be in a plane which has just made a crash landing and caught fire?! No doubt some people have other travel connections to make or relatives waiting to meet them whom they haven't seen for years. But for everyone who may have some semblance of an excuse there must be many who are being nothing more than plain selfish.

The same kind of undignified scramble disturbed the Lord Jesus one day when He attended a feast. It was customary for careful seating arrangements to be made at the banquets held in those days. The guests would recline at one side of small tables set for three people. All the tables were arranged to form a large U. The place of honor was in the center place of the

111

table at the base of the U, with the most honorable seats being to the right and left of the guest of honor. Then the tables nearest the base of the U were filled until the least honorable places on the wings of the U were occupied.

On the occasion mentioned in Scripture Jesus noticed the guests were scrambling over each other in a most undignified attempt to secure for themselves the best possible place. This prompted Him to tell a parable designed to expose their selfishness, to teach basic good manners and to introduce them to an elementary course in etiquette.

Selfishness or Self-Respect

Before we get into a study of the parable it would be good if we could clarify the situation about selfishness. It is obvious from Scripture that people are required to have a healthy attitude towards themselves. We have concentrated on such passages of Scripture as "What a wretched man I am!" (Rom. 7:24) and produced a strange kind of humility of which we have sometimes been paradoxically proud. This has been proven to me on numerous occasions when I have responded to such protestations by saying, "Right on, you're a real first class creep!" only to find that the person concerned was insulted by my agreement! Like the lady in Texas who, after telling me that she had done something silly, asked me, "Would you believe that a woman of my age and education, breeding and upbringing could do such a stupid thing?" "Oh yes," I replied "I have no difficulty believing that at all!" She got very upset with me!

There is no doubt that when we consider our inability to live as we would desire and as we have been encouraged we, like Paul, should be constantly humbled before the Lord. But we should not lose sight of the fact that we are required to "love our neighbor as ourselves" (see Luke 10:27) which, whatever else it means, certainly insists that we should have a healthy sense of self-respect and encourage and protect our neighbor as he seeks to develop a similar attitude. Selfishness is far removed from the healthy self-respect that God requires us to have and which He expects us to promote in terms of attitudes to other people.

To care for my self-preservation is not only a built-in reflex, as anyone who has narrowly escaped death at the hands of a Filipino taxi driver will readily testify, but also a mature attitude towards myself as a special piece of divine creation. To care enough to keep myself clean and tidy is to have a kind of self-respect which indicates that carelessness and laziness are incompatible with my profession that I serve the living and true God.

Selfishness—Disregard for God and Man

Selfishness is much more subtle than these things. It is an attitude that challenges God's right to be God and individuals' rights to be individuals when they, that is both God and individuals, come within the sphere of my influence. Selfishness doesn't want to do what God wants if what God wants is incompatible with selfishness' plans. Selfishness cares not for the needs and aspirations of others whenever they come into close proximity with the needs and aspirations of self. Accordingly, both God and people are relegated to a position of relative unimportance as the selfish person places himself in the place of supreme importance.

To push past someone disembarking from a plane is to say, "Don't you realize I have a prior right to get off this plane ahead of you because I happen to be

113

more important than you." To rush to a concert early to get the best seats is to say, "For reasons that only I know I deserve the best seats more than anyone else in this place." To deny God the things He rightly claims for Himself and to use them on ourselves is to selfishly disobey God and indicate that we feel comfortable placing ourselves in a position where this attitude is justifiable!

Webster's Dictionary defines *selfishness* as "the exclusive consideration by a person of his own interest and happiness." The exclusiveness being demonstrated in both disregard for man and disobedience to God. So in effect selfishness is the deifying of self. As the guests were assembling for the dinner party the Master saw a man who was suffering from dropsy. No doubt the poor man had taken steps to put himself in the path of the Lord hoping that He might have compassion on him. There is little doubt that the Pharisees were rather glad to see him there too. Not that they were particularly concerned that he should be healed but rather because they realized that Jesus might go ahead and heal him on the Sabbath day, thereby starting the next round in the ongoing battle that had been going on with Him on the subject of healing on the Sabbath.

Apparently recognizing what the Pharisees and "experts in the law" were thinking, the Lord took the initiative and asked the old, old question, "Is it lawful to heal on the Sabbath day or not?" When they did not answer He went ahead and healed the man adding words similar to those He spoke when He healed the woman who had been crippled for 18 years. This time however, He added the thought that the Sabbatarians were not so committed to the concept of no work on the Sabbath that they would leave their son or ox in an empty well if they fell in on the special

114

day. (It is interesting to note that some versions say "son" and others "donkey," presumably demonstrating that the problem of distinguishing between the two is not a new one!)

Principles and Pride

There are two illustrations of selfishness in this incident. The people, who were prepared to let a person suffer for the sake of a principle of man's making, were saying that their concepts of right and wrong were to be guarded at all costs even if they were unable to give an unequivocal answer to the Lord's question inquiring about the legality of their position. The inability to answer and the silence that followed the question are both indicative of their own uncertainty. And it would be reasonable to assume that people in such a precarious position would have been glad to surrender an indefensible point for the sake of the man's well-being. This, however, was not to be the case because concern for their moral rectitude and social acceptance outweighed all other considerations.

Bearing this in mind, it is particularly striking to note that these people were not totally inflexible. When it was a matter of their own well-being or that of those close to them, they were quite comfortable changing their position and making room in their laws for their self-interests to be safeguarded. This again is so blatantly selfish that it must have been in the forefront of the Master's mind as He went into the dining room and was confronted with the sight of the people jostling for position.

The consuming desire to get what we want and to be where we think we ought to be is so powerful that we often succumb to it without even beginning to think of the seriousness of what we are doing. To get the best seat for myself is a clear commentary on my own self-evaluation. "I am the greatest so where is the greatest seat?" But it is also a commentary on my evaluation of everyone else in the room. "Because I am superior they are obviously inferior." The only way I can upgrade myself is at the expense of other people because the whole value system operating in a room full of jostling people is a system that operates on the relative worth of each person to the other. Therefore the conclusion that I deserve and shall have the best seat is arrived at by my upgrading through everyone else's degrading.

It has always been a cause of mystification to me that in our pragmatic world everyone loves a winner but has little time for a loser. Why are we so high on winners and so down on losers when we can't possibly have one without the other? It takes a loser to manufacture a winner. Or do we think that we can be exalted in the competitive world without the exaltation being at someone else's expense? To decide that my upgrading, at the expense of the other person's degrading, is justified, is to demonstrate a remarkable degree of selfishness.

The words of the Master "Take the lowest place" must have fallen on many red ears! His reminder that those who take the high place always run the risk of being unceremoniously bundled out of it to a lower place must have been exactly the sort of thing they didn't want to hear because it meant that somebody thought they were not as important as they undoubtedly were!

Ministry or Fellowship

Warming to His theme, the Lord then gave His host some more helpful hints on how to give a dinner party. "Don't fill your dinner parties with people you

116

know will invite you back to their parties. If you do this you are not having any ministry to people, you are simply having a good time with your friends." We should be careful not to misunderstand the Lord at this point. He was not speaking out against the delights of fellowship and sharing with those we love, because we know that He enjoyed the hospitality of Lazarus and his two sisters and apparently was not averse to attending a good dinner party on occasions. He was pointing out to the prominent Pharisee that he should realize that his entertaining was not going to count as a ministry to the needy because there weren't any needy there. Therefore he should recognize the necessity for inviting "the poor, the crippled, the lame and the blind."

Jesus, by saying this put His finger on another sore, selfish spot. There is no doubt that most of us would much prefer to entertain those we like and who like us than to go out on a limb and open our homes and our lives to those we don't know and, even if we did know, probably wouldn't like! Rather than risk such an unpleasant experience we leave the needy in their need and go ahead with our pleasant, unthreatening engagements, perhaps thereby demonstrating the same old selfishness all over again.

The Master's remarks on the subject of issuing invitations to dinner parties were listened to by all those within earshot. When He told His host quite bluntly that he had better get all the reward he could from his parties by being invited to the parties of his friends because there certainly would not be any eternal reward for him, one of the listeners burst out, "Blessed is the man who will eat at the feast in the kingdom of God." This prompted the Master to embark on another brief parable also related to feasts and invitations.

The Parable of the Great Banquet

This time He talked about the man who invited friends to his party. They agreed to come and when he sent his servant to tell them dinner was served they all started to make excuses. We should remember that while this system sounds very strange to us, it was normal in the days of the Lord. The people had no watches so the invitations would not specify an hour. Preparations also took a considerable amount of time so the only way to make sure the people arrived on time was to get everything ready and then round them up!

The change of mind by the guests was therefore inexcusable. They had indicated their glad acceptance, and on this basis the host had prepared the meal which now would be totally wasted. The host, however, rather than waste the meal sent word out to all the needy people that they could have a free meal. But even after they were all packed into the house there was still room so the host sent out his servants again to hunt out all the destitute people living in the hedgeways and highways and insist that they come.

The inference in this parable is that those who were first invited into the Kingdom and refused should realize that the door is now open wide for all to come in and enjoy the delicacies of God's provision and the benefits of His grace. The selfishness of those who initially accepted and later changed their minds is so obvious it hardly needs to be commented upon. But the fact that they gave excuses that were palpably unsatisfactory adds insult to injury. Not a reason was mentioned, only excuses. So they not only showed their disinterest in the waste they had caused, the embarrassment they piled on their host, and the fact that their word was not their bond, but they also demonstrated that their host didn't even merit a genuine honest word from them. This again was an insulting degrading of one man for the personal convenience of another. Selfishness is the best word to describe it.

The Consequences of Selfishness

Selfish people, because they are so selfish, ought to be most interested in the consequences of their selfishness. The Master taught that selfish people will experience certain things themselves. They will suffer embarrassment when their selfishness is exposed in the society in which it has been exercised. Having taken their high seat they will be moved to the lowest seat. The very thought of such humiliation ought to give every selfish person cause for careful thought.

The statement of principle by the Master to the effect that "everyone who exalts himself will be humbled, and he who humbles himself will be exalted," ought to serve as a reminder to those whose sole interest is their well-being that only those who take the humble place can anticipate the exalted position in the divine evaluation.

Furthermore the eternal aspect of the selfish lifestyle should not be overlooked, because not only will the person who has deified himself be left destitute in the great Resurrection Day but, according to the parable of the dinner party, those who ignore the invitation to respond to the King's gracious offer of blessing should realize "not one of those men ... will get a taste of my banquet."

In a world where selfishness is accepted as normal, and self-indulgence has to be encouraged for the sake of sales and increased productivity, it is difficult to get people to recognize how desperate is the condition of the unrepentantly selfish person. That person is not normal; he is lost in his misguided pride and misbegotten greed which have produced his selfishness. His misplaced love for himself and his mistaken evaluation of the people God has created, all lead to the inevitable disaster that all those who have reserved the divine order must anticipate.

Selfishness Is Sin

There is of course always the opportunity to repent of selfishness and come humbly before the Lord freely admitting that selfishness is sin and needs to be forgiven. Because God is replaced by self, the command to "love the Lord thy God and to have no other gods before Him" is clearly broken. And, because selfishness degrades the other member of society who suffers the effects of the selfishness, the command "to love thy neighbor as thyself" is also clearly disobeyed. Therein lies the sin and therefore repentance is necessary. Once repentance has been entered into it needs to be maintained as an attitude because selfishness is always with us and the temptation to revert to the old life-style comes with every choice that comes our way. The capacity to cope with the ongoing decisions to reject the self-life and replace it with the life of humble service has to be discovered through a deepening relationship with Christ Himself.

His example of unselfish service and sacrificial lifestyle has to be deeply engrained in the consciousness of the believer. A desire to emulate this style of living has to be born and then the necessary sacrificial steps have to be taken.

When I was a young boy I heard a well-known American preacher, Donald Grey Barnhouse, speak at the famous Keswick Convention in England. He was an imposing figure and I remember his clear loud voice as he stood before the congregation and boomed, "The way to up is down." Pausing for dramatic effect he then went on. "And the way to down is up." At that point I clearly remember giving up on him because, to my youthful mind, it was quite impossible for me to understand a man who was so confused. Years later I suddenly realized that he had been putting in pithy form the words of the Master which other scriptural writers repeated on a number of occasions.

If I had listened to Dr. Barnhouse I would have saved myself a lot of wasted time spent on selfish pursuits. I would have recognized the folly of being my own god while professing that God was my God. And countless people would have been spared the humiliation of being treated incorrectly by me in my selfishness.

To recognize the force and the consequencs of selfishness is to be alerted to the most common and possibly the most destructive power at work in society today. It behooves the believer to insure that his eyes are set on the goal of being like Christ, and his heart is set on drawing from the gracious enabling of the Spirit whatever it takes to say no to selfishness and yes to that which He would have us do.

Shortly after being introduced to the things of which I have written in this chapter I was also introduced to a hymn which has since become a great favorite because it voices a great desire of my redeemed heart:

> O to be saved from myself dear Lord,
> O to be lost in Thee,
> O that it might be no more "I"
> But "Christ who lives in me."

10 Lostness— Challenge to Churches

Luke 15:1-32—The Lost Sheep, Coin, and Son

Now the tax collectors and "sinners" were all gathering around to hear him. But the Pharisees and the teachers of the law muttered, "This man welcomes sinners and eats with them."

Then Jesus told them this parable: "Suppose one of you has a hundred sheep and loses one of them. Does he not leave the ninety-nine in the open country and go after the lost sheep until he finds it? And when he finds it, he joyfully puts it on his shoulders and goes home. Then he calls his friends and neighbors together and says, 'Rejoice with me; I have found my lost sheep.' I tell you that in the same way there is more rejoicing in heaven over one sinner who repents than over ninety-nine righteous persons who do not need to repent.

"Or suppose a woman has ten silver coins and loses one. Does she not light a lamp, sweep the house and search carefully until she finds it? And when she finds it, she calls her friends and neighbors together and says, 'Rejoice with me; I have found my lost coin.' In the same way, I tell you, there is rejoicing in the presence of the angels of God over one sinner who repents."

Jesus continued: "There was a man who had two sons. The younger one said to his father, 'Father, give me my share of the estate.' So he divided his property between them.

"Not long after that, the younger son got together all he had, set off for a distant country and there squandered his wealth in wild living. After he had spent everything, there was a severe famine in that whole country, and he began to be in need. So he went and hired himself out to a citizen of that country, who sent him to his fields to feed pigs. He longed to fill his stomach with the pods that the pigs were eating, but no one gave him anything.

"When he came to his senses, he said, 'How many of my father's hired men have food to spare, and here I am starving to death! I will set out and go back to my father and say to him: Father, I have sinned against heaven and against you. I am no longer worthy to be called your son; make me like one of your hired men.' So he got up and went to his father.

"But while he was still a long way off, his father saw him and was filled with compassion for him; he ran to his son, threw his arms around him and kissed him.

"The son said to him, 'Father, I have sinned against heaven and against you. I am no longer worthy to be called your son.'

"But the father said to his servants, 'Quick! Bring the best robe and put it on him. Put a ring on his

123

*finger and sandals on his feet. Bring the fattened calf
and kill it. Let's have a feast and celebrate. For this
son of mine was dead and is alive again; he was lost
and is found.' So they began to celebrate.*

"*Meanwhile, the older son was in the field. When he
came near the house he heard music and dancing. So
he called one of the servants and asked him what was
going on. 'Your brother has come,' he replied, 'and
your father has killed the fattened calf because he has
him back safe and sound.'*

"*The older brother became angry and refused to go
in. So his father went out and pleaded with him. But
he answered his father, 'Look! All these years I've been
slaving for you and never disobeyed your orders. Yet
you never gave me even a young goat so I could celebrate with my friends. But when this son of yours who
has squandered your property with prostitutes comes
home, you kill the fattened calf for him!'*

" '*My son,' the father said, 'you are always with me,
and everything I have is yours. But we had to celebrate
and be glad, because this brother of yours was dead
and is alive again; he was lost and is found.'*"

The bright young man in the bright new sports car
braked to an impressive screeching halt alongside the
old country man sitting outside his English pub, puff-
ing contentedly on his pipe.

"I say, old man, can you direct me to Taunton?"

"No."

"Surely you know where Taunton is. Which direction do I take?"

"I told you I don't know."

"Well how far am I from Tavistock?"

"Don't know."

"Which direction is Tavistock."

"Don't rightly know."

"You don't know much, do you?" said the young man by this time totally exasperated with the old-timer.

"No, I don't, but I'm not lost!"

Some people, like the young man in the story, know a lot about a lot of things but are so lost that their knowledge is of little value to them. Others like the old man make little profession to know much but at least they know enough to make sure they aren't lost. This at least gives them the freedom to use what knowledge they have!

One of the main criticisms to which Christ was subjected was that He seemed to enjoy the company of those whom He ought really to have been avoiding, according to the rules of the game as issued by the religious hierarchy of His day. Constantly His critics reiterated the accusation, "This man welcomes sinners and eats with them." We need to be sympathetic to the concerns of the leadership because it is incumbent on those who seek to honor the Lord to make sure that their life-style contrasts sharply with those who have no concern to live before Him.

This contrast can best be maintained in some circumstances by withdrawal from that which is regarded as incompatible with godly living and even detrimental to the ones seeking to be godly. But this attitude can be carried so far that those who would be different become so engrossed in their position that they become isolated from those who are in the other position. This is not satisfactory and whenever believers adopt a position toward those who are godless that puts isolation in the place of biblical separation, both believers and unbelievers will suffer. The tension was best resolved by the Master Himself. At no time did He isolate Himself from sinners but at no time did He associate with their sin.

Participation in Lostness

His reason for spending time with the godless was that He regarded them as being lost. This He made very clear when He told a series of parables designed to answer the criticism. First He expressed the feelings of a shepherd who, after losing one of his sheep, spends time looking for it in the wilderness, finds it, and returns home rejoicing with the lost sheep on his shoulders. Then Jesus emphasized His point by telling about the little woman who lost a silver coin and stopped everything until she had cleaned the house thoroughly so that she could find her missing money.

He then went even further and related what is probably the best known of all His parables, the story of the prodigal son.

This story relates the incident of a young man who takes the money and runs. He then proceeds to waste the money, become totally estranged from his family and arrive at destitution and disaster. At which point he "came to his senses," returned home and heard his father say among other things, "he was lost and is found, let's celebrate!"

The Greek word *apollumi*, which is translated "lost" in Luke 15:24, is also used in other ways in the same Gospel. This multiple usage is helpful because it allows us to see the richness of ideas which were included in the term. For example when the Lord had His conflict with the demon-possessed man in Capernaum, as recorded in chapter 4, the demon said, "Have you come to destroy us?" The word *destroy* is equivalent to the word *lost.* Lostness means destruction.

Then one day when talking to some people who evidently thought that He and His disciples were not taking things as seriously as they might, particularly when compared to John the Baptist and the Pharisees, the Lord answered by talking about patching old clothes and filling old wineskins. He pointed out that old clothes patched with new pieces don't hold together and old wineskins filled with new wine disintegrate. The same Greek word, *apollumi* is used in this sense. So we see that *lostness* also means *disintegration.*

When speaking to His special group of disciples in an effort to impress upon them the magnitude of their commitment to Him and His to them He reminded them that it was easy for people to hold on to their lives and thus eventually lose them. But if they would be prepared to invest their lives in Him they would find reality in life. But the choice confronting them was whether they would waste their lives on themselves and finish up with nothing of eternal significance, or "waste" their lives on Him and arrive in eternity with treasure already laid up for them. To lose in this sense means to waste and so the word *lostness* includes the idea of *dissipation.*

Participation in Discovery

When we come to the parables of the lost sheep, the lost coin and the lost son it is easy to see that each of the lost items, while clearly different from each other, had in common the fact that they were estranged from their ideal environment and experiencing some degree of disorientation.

Translated into the experience of people whom we all know it is not difficult to recognize those who are suffering lostness. The sense of disorientation is one of the most common things that people talk to me about in counseling. People from all walks of life tell me that they have a sense of unreality, that something is out of whack, that they feel as if something indefinable is wrong with their lives. They have a sensation that they are not part of a whole, they are unrelated to what is going on around them. Unsure of who they are, confused as to their proper role as humans, they complain that they apparently are achieving less than they think they should. But they are not sure what they should be accomplishing! This sense of dissipation of life, wasting of energy, and squandering of opportunity is leading to frustration and concern. Worried about what they are, where they are, where they are going, what they are doing, they see life slipping away, days rushing into weeks and weeks becoming years without any feeling of achievement and ultimate success.

Those of us who spend time dealing with people are well aware of the fact that New Year's Day is a time when many people go into depression. Last New Year's Day I had a number of calls from people who commenced their conversation by saying that they hoped they weren't disturbing me on a holiday or interrupting my time with my family, *BUT*, and then they launched into a description of their futility and a litany of their lostness. The consciousness that another year had passed was underlining their lostness.

At the root of this malady is the sense of disintegration. The word had come to mean "falling apart" or "coming apart at the seams" which is of course quite accurate. But it should be remembered that disintegration has to do with a lack of integration. The integrating point of a wheel is the hub. The integrating point of man is God. Hubless wheels buckle and collapse, godless men do the same thing. The disorientation, destruction and dissipation are all related to disintegration. All these big words spell *lost*.

The little woman who lost her coin certainly didn't want to lose it, neither did the coin want to get lost! But when certain circumstances come into the experience of a coin, lostness becomes practically inevitable. If the coin is placed on the table along with a number of other things it's only a matter of time until someone with a tidy mind puts everything in order but inadvertently knocks the coin off the edge. Gravity takes over and the coin falls. Because it is circular the coin rolls. Because the floor slopes it rolls down into a corner. Because the light is in the middle of the room it rolls into the shade. Because it lies in the shade it gets lost. One inevitable thing after another leads to its lostness.

Sheep however are different. They have a whole lot more in their makeup than coins. Sheep have a tendency to wander, particularly if they are not well fed, or if someone leaves a gate open. Coins have no way of knowing that they are lost but all those who have lost sheep know that sheep soon recognize that they are in trouble and bleat accordingly.

While there is a difference in the causes of lostness in the case of coins and sheep, there is a major difference between lost people and lost coins and sheep. If coins get lost through circumstances that they are unable to control and sheep get lost through a well-developed tendency to wander, men get lost through choice. The young man in the famous story carefully planned his lostness from his family. It was something he desired and achieved. For reasons that are not given he had determined to disassociate himself from his family and strike out on his own.

In the spiritual realm, which of course was the concern of the Master when He told the parables, people are lost and there is a sense in which the experience of the coin is similar to theirs. Circumstances abound to enable people to go wrong. Educational systems, starting with misguided parents, perpetuated by godless educators and humanistic higher educators, often place young people in an environment where their lostness is almost as predictable as the lostness of the coin.

It would be wrong however for us to think that humans are like inanimate coins whose fate is determined by circumstances quite outside their control. That there are determining factors can hardly be denied but to believe in a crude determinism leading to inevitable lostness does justice neither to human experience nor biblical truth.

There is a sheepishness about mankind that was spotlighted by Isaiah's well known simile, "We all, like sheep have gone astray." While external circumstances play their part the internal disposition to wandering that is so clearly demonstrated in human behavior must not be overlooked. But it is in the clear presentation of the lostness of the young man that we recognize that, whatever the external circumstance or the internal disposition, men and women get lost ultimately because they choose to be lost. There is something about individual freedom from God that attracts them more than the benefits of home. The lure of a life-style dedicated to personal indulgence is more powerful than the pull of a life-style devoted to the service of God. The choice to turn to our own way is therefore understandable if not excusable. And those who make the choice to disassociate with God, do so fully understanding what they are doing, although they may not be aware that they are choosing disorientation and disintegration as well.

Involvement of Heavenly Seeker

The attitude of the Master to this universal state of lostness was clearly chronicled by His actions as well as His words. Spending a considerable amount of time with the lost in order that He might reach them, led to a great blessing in those whom He found even though it opened Him up to grave misunderstanding and criticism. Like the woman who lost the coin, He devoted Himself to a persistent search for those who were so lost that they were apparently incapable of articulating their lostness. The man lying incapable and disconsolate at the pool of Bethesda was like a lost coin. But the Master took the initiative and got to him where he was. But not all lost ones lie in the shade. Some, like the blind man of Jericho, bleat loud and clear when the Good Shepherd gets within earshot. And He hears and answers their cry for help.

The personal and persistent aspects of God's search for lost people, illustrated by the woman cleaning the house and the Shepherd searching the hills, bring untold encouragement to the lost who have been found. Not until they were found did they begin to suspect that the Lord had been working on their behalf in innumerable ways for a long time. But once found they realized that their foundness was related to God's faithfulness.

There is another side to the situation as illustrated by the parable of the prodigal. In his case the father stayed at home and waited for the son to "come to his senses." Comforting as it is to know that the Father takes the initiative in seeking the lost we should never forget the necessity for lost people, once alerted to their condition, to take the necessary steps to reconciliation. These steps include willingness to call lostness by its proper name. The young man in the pigpen could conceivably have blamed his condition on the famine, his boss, the inhospitable people or even the pigs and the pods, but he was the responsible person. To admit responsibility requires an admittance of muddled thinking and bad deciding, in short, a self-humbling. The humbling comes to a climax when we return to the one from whom we have become estranged, and this is never an easy thing to do.

But perhaps the hardest and most humbling thing is the recognition that, having chosen independence of God which led to lostness, those who are found have to embark on a life-style of dependence. The young son who charted his own course, and designed his own downfall, had to come with empty hands and not only receive what he didn't deserve from a gracious Father but he had to submit himself to a new responsibility as a son of the Father.

The Master insisted that He was seeking the lost but also that the lost must seek the Father. Those who seek with all their hearts, find. This applies not only to the seeking lost ones but also to the seeking Father, through the Son.

Joy in Discovery of Reconciliation

The involvement of the Son in this ministry is beautifully expressed in each parable by the emphasis on *rejoicing* in each case. To Him the seeking of the lost is a delight and the consummation of the search a cause for celebration. It was particularly hard for Him, therefore, to accept the attitude of those who had no conception of what He was doing or no interest in being involved themselves.

This brings us to another aspect of lostness that we should not miss. So far we have considered the participation of the lost person both in his lostness and his discovery, and the involvement of the heavenly seeker and His ultimate joy in discovery and reconciliation. But the thrust of the three parables is surely that God's people should be intimately concerned with the condition of lost people and practically involved in reaching them.

132

Some, like the Pharisees, are exclusively concerned with preserving their own purity and maintaining their own integrity. Purity and integrity are legitimate causes for concern but not at the expense of the lost. This is perfectly clear, as we have seen, from the example of the Saviour. To understand this is to be challenged to develop a base of purity and integrity so strong that it will not be jeopardized by involvement with those whose integrity has been prostituted and whose purity is tarnished.

From a practical point of view I firmly believe that individuals who embark on ministries to those who are in the depths of lostness, without building safeguards into their ministry, are being at best unwise and at worst irresponsible. For instance I have great concerns for those people who specialize in a counseling ministry that involves hours and hours of dealing with broken marriages, sexual problems and lonely vulnerable people of the opposite sex. Some seekers of such lost people have not been as concerned with their own purity and integrity as they ought to have been and those who have a pastoral concern have failed in their overseeing ministry to the counselors. As a result not a few counselors and ministers have agreed to compromising situations which have led even to the point of destruction of the ministry. This should not happen if proper safeguards are built into the ministries of those who will not accept either the separatism of the Pharisee or the carelessness of the reckless.

Concern with the Lost

The attitude of the elder brother is somewhat different. He was not particularly concerned with his own position except as it was challenged by the return of his younger brother and the attention which was given to the returned prodigal presumably at his expense. Frankly he didn't think that people as lost as his brother had any rights to the family blessings and he was not reticent to express his disapproval of the father's generosity. This was nothing more than rank prejudice and infantile pettiness. But before we condemn him too summarily we should search our own ecclesiastical heart to see if there is perhaps something of this behind the church's apparent uninvolvement in a seeking ministry.

There are, as we all know, churches that make no attempt to reach the lost because church people disapprove so thoroughly of their behavior. To reach such people and then to bring them to the church services and integrate such people into the church family would mean exposing everybody to certain challenging and perhaps painful experiences. In fact churches have fallen so far from a concern to reach those who have not been brought up in the Christian subculture and who do not accordingly behave Christianly, that even those who do not belong to churches don't expect churches to have such people in their fold.

This has been brought home to me on numerous occasions. Some years ago when we were planning to move our church premises the neighbors in the new area objected at a public meeting saying, "We don't want this kind of church in our vicinity because they will bring undesirables into the neighborhood." We agreed but couldn't understand what kind of church would not be attracting "undesirables." A few days ago at another hearing, which was called to deal with the unfortunate situation caused by our Sunday morning traffic blocking the freeway, one man testified, "Some of the people who attend that church aren't very religious when it comes to driving." We agreed but tried to show him that those kind of people were the very kind we were trying to get to! Another man called me to say, "My daughter will not be attending your church anymore, because you have so many strange people there." I replied, "You're right. Thanks for the compliment. Like our Master we're seeking the lost and hope never to stop till He says, 'Enough!' "

11 Shrewdness—The Way to Eternal Dwellings

Luke 16:1-13—The Shrewd Manager

Jesus told his disciples: "There was a rich man whose manager was accused of wasting his possessions. So he called him in and asked him, 'What is this I hear about you? Give an account of your management, because you cannot be manager any longer.'

"The manager said to himself, 'What shall I do now? My master is taking away my job. I'm not strong enough to dig, and I'm ashamed to beg—I know what I'll do so that, when I lose my job here, people will welcome me into their houses.'

"So he called in each one of his master's debtors. He asked the first, 'How much do you owe my master?'

" 'Eight hundred gallons of olive oil,' he replied.

"The manager told him, 'Take your bill, sit down quickly, and make it four hundred.'

"Then he asked the second, 'And how much do you owe?'

" 'A thousand bushels of wheat,' he replied.

"He told him, 'Take your bill and make it eight hundred.'

"The master commended the dishonest manager because he had acted shrewdly. For the people of this world are more shrewd in dealing with their own kind than are the people of the light. I tell you, use worldly wealth to gain friends for yourselves, so that when it is gone, you will be welcomed into eternal dwellings.

"Whoever can be trusted with very little can also be trusted with much, and whoever is dishonest with very little will also be dishonest with much. So if you have not been trustworthy in handling worldly wealth, who will trust you with true riches? And if you have not been trustworthy with someone else's property, who will give you property of your own?"

Good men sometimes do good things badly. Neville Chamberlain is a good example. When he went off to Munich to see Adolf Hitler in the turbulent days before World War II he undoubtedly was a good man who only wanted peace. He came back from Munich triumphantly waving his piece of paper proclaiming, "Peace in our time." But there were those who knew that even as he proclaimed "Peace," he had misread Hitler and mismanaged the situation. Subsequent events showed conclusively that he was a good man wanting only to do good but he handled it badly.

Bad men sometimes do bad things well. The Great Train Robbery certainly proved this to be true. The men involved were bad men as their willingness to hurt innocent people and their readiness to rob clearly demonstrated. Their actions were wrong as everyone agreed, but strange as it may seem these bad men became some kind of folk heroes. Even people committed to "law and order" expressed grudging admiration for them. The reason being that they had done a marvelous job! The brilliance of their conception, the care of their preparation, the skill of the execution of their plan, and their expertise in salting away the funds stolen and submerging themselves in foreign cultures all spoke to the fact that these bad men did a bad thing well.

Sometimes we don't want to admit these things. Perhaps we feel that we should defend the good men as if their basic goodness or their well-meaning intent would be disqualified if they were ever recognized as being humans capable of error. And we are reluctant to admit that bad men can ever do anything well in case we appear to be excusing their badness and condoning their actions. Jesus, however, felt no such reservations. He was not only prepared to admit that bad men do bad things well, He was prepared to use them as illustrations!

The Shrewd Manager

Apparently, Jesus was concerned that His disciples were being a little too naive. So He told them a parable about the manager of a household who got himself fired. When his boss called him in to deliver the bad news the manager realized he would need to act quickly because he had no means of supporting himself. He briefly considered getting a job digging ditches but decided that was too much like work. He dismissed begging because, although it wasn't work, it was too humbling. Then he had a great idea! He reckoned that as he couldn't beg and wouldn't work his only mèans of support was charity. But he had no means of knowing who would be charitable to him so he decided to put some people in a position so that they would feel obligated to be charitable!

There was one man who owed his boss more than 800 gallons of olive oil. He called the man in and said, "Take your bill, sit down quickly, and make it four hundred." Then warming to his task he sent for another debtor who owed his boss a lot of wheat.

He asked him, "How much do you owe?"

"A thousand bushels of wheat."

"Take your bill and make it eight hundred."

Both the oil man and the wheat man didn't need telling twice and off they went with their altered bills, rejoicing in their good fortune and thanking their lucky stars for such a crooked manager!

Shortly afterwards the boss found out what his manager had done and surprisingly, "The master commended the dishonest manager because he had acted shrewdly." Many modern-day disciples wish the Lord hadn't told this story because they feel that He was condoning the actions of the crooked manager. However, if the parable is read carefully, it is clear that it was the master who did the commending, not the Master! In no way did the Lord give His seal of approval to the crooked manager's dishonesty and we should not necessarily assume that his boss did either. Some people think that the boss commended the manager very grudgingly in much the same way that law-abiding citizens of Britain grudgingly commended the men who pulled off the Great Train Robbery. But others have pointed out that there was a common practice in business circles in the Lord's day that was not exactly ethical but a lot of people did it anyway.

There was an old prohibition on charging interest on loans in those days. This was intended to protect the helpless from the unscrupulous! Some businessmen, understandably, didn't like this very much so they did what businessmen have been known to do on other occasions. They found a way around the law! They didn't charge interest they just billed people for more than they gave them. So, for instance, the man whose bill was altered from a thousand bushels to eight hundred may have only borrowed eight hundred and the extra two hundred was in lieu of interest.

The boss was put in a real fix when he discovered what had happened. If he objected and told the manager to alter the bills back to the original figure he would be open to exposure as someone who charged interest without charging it! On the other hand, he must have been furious that his rascally manager had outwitted him so easily. After considering the situation he decided that he would rather protect his reputation than get even with his manager so he put a good face on and said, "Well done, my man. I'm glad to see that you are wanting to conform to the law."

Shrewd as Snakes

Whichever interpretation is correct we know that the manager was certainly a crook but he was a shrewd crook! And the Lord Jesus felt that His men needed to sharpen up in the area of shrewdness. He stated that "the people of this world are more shrewd in dealing with their own kind than are the people of light." On another occasion the Master found it necessary to say a similar thing to His disciples. When He was busy warning them of the perils of being His disciples in a predominantly hostile world He told them that it would be necessary for them to be "as shrewd as snakes and as innocent as doves" (Matt. 10:16). I've never been able to get close enough to snakes to tell how shrewd they are, but the same expression is used to describe the tactics of Satan in his role as serpent in the Garden.

Ezekiel in his prophetic statement on Jehovah's behalf against the ruler of Tyre said, "By your wisdom and understanding you have gained wealth for yourself and amassed gold and silver in your treasuries" (Ezek. 28:4).

He used the same word as the one used of Satan in Genesis which is related to the ideas expressed both on the parable and the Lord's "shrewd as snakes" remark. This helps us to understand what it was that the Lord was conscious His disciples lacked and what He wanted to see them build into their character.

The shrewdness of the manager was clearly expressed in the way he was able to size up his situation in a flash. Quicker than it takes to tell he had worked out his predicament, considered alternatives and arrived at the conclusion that he was well and truly caught! That was good thinking and disciples of Christ need to be able to size up their situations quickly too. Sometimes they go blundering into situations that they would avoid like the plague if they thought about what they were getting into. For example, some disciples of Christ engage in marvelous discussions with unbelievers without realizing that the more they talk the more they dig a hole for their arguments and a grave for their testimony!

Action Not Meditation

The manager was also astute enough to realize that he needed action not meditation! The classic evangelical response to many urgent pleas for help or pressing calls for action is, "I'll pray about it!" At the risk of appearing to be totally heretical, I would have to say that the above response is often more of statement of indecisiveness than a statement of faith.

141

When one talks in that tone of voice it may sound pious but it may also denote incompetence.

The ability to recognize personal strengths and weaknesses is another thing that the manager exhibited. He knew he had little chance of making a living as a ditchdigger. He had no illusions about his chances as a professional beggar and he knew instinctively that his only assets were intangible and invisible. Therefore, he needed to test the water and see how much support he could expect from the debtors and take his chance at improving whatever support he could find.

The disciples of Christ have a peculiar tendency either to be unaware or unconcerned about their strengths and weaknesses. For strange reasons they seem to be very happy to let people who can't do things, do them, while those who can, sit idly by. George Bernard Shaw's well known adage, "Those who can, do, those who can't, teach" sometimes doesn't apply to the "people of light." For them it is, "Those who can, don't, those who can't, preach."

Then the manager showed a remarkable ability to act quickly once he had determined his course of action.

Believers have good reason to act expeditiously considering the sense of urgency in all that Christ did and taught and the fact that world need and opportunity are growing apace all the time. But unfortunately this is far from the case. The structure of many churches which allows for all kinds of people to have all manner of input is certainly helpful in making "people feel part of what is going on." But it is no way to get things done that ought to be done. A few days ago I was given a little plaque for my desk which said, "God so loved the world He didn't send a committee." I realize the need for good committee work and the nurturing of the body of believers, but I think that we should learn that shrewd people act quickly when the time is ripe and the people of light ought to have things so set up that they can do likewise.

Be Shrewd in Handling Mammon

Having made His powerful point about shrewdness the Master proceeded to talk to His disciples about being shrewd in their handling of *mammon*. The word *mammon* has not found its way into the English language other than in the Bible so it is necessary for us to be clear what it is, particularly if we have some of it and are told to use it wisely! It is an Aramaic word which means wealth or possessions. Jesus called it "unrighteous mammon" not because wealth is by definition sinful, but because wealth is sometimes accumulated by less than ethical means.

Without any apparent embarrassment the Master told His disciples that they were not handling their finances properly and He expected to see them being much more astute in their stewardship. He drew a clear parallel between "worldly wealth" and "true riches" and showed that a person's spiritual condition can sometimes be more accurately diagnosed by his financial involvement than by anything else. He insisted that those believers who are untrustworthy in their financial dealings will not be trusted with anything of spiritual significance.

Then Jesus added His reasoning which was that if you can't be trusted with a little you can't be trusted with a lot. Money in comparison to eternal riches is little, so if you can't handle it properly don't figure on handling too much of the real stuff! His climactic comment was that if you can't be trusted to handle someone else's property for them you shouldn't expect that person to give you some property for yourself. The application being that God has loaned you all the assets you possess in order that they might be rightly handled to further His purposes and if we mishandle this assignment we should not expect any great eternal rewards from Him!

You Cannot Serve God and Money

From the limited accounts we have of the Lord's earthly situation it would appear that He lived on the edge of poverty, certainly by the standards that we regard as normal. He was, however, constantly warning people of the incipient dangers of wealth. To the wealthy He spoke of greed and avarice. To the poor He spoke of envy and jealousy. Those who had wealth would have to be aware that they might become unscrupulous in their efforts to keep it. Those who didn't have it must be alert to the dangers of taking illegitimate steps to gain it or entertaining illegitimate attitudes towards it.

To the Master there was always the great awareness that if people don't handle their money, their money will handle them. His way of stating this is short and to the point. "You cannot serve God and money." When money becomes so overpoweringly important that we are caught up in the business of getting it and keeping it we have come to the point of serving it, even though we may even subscribe to the popular notion that we are making our money serve us! The only way to avoid this is to recognize it is an either/or situation. Either God is God of you and your money, or money is your god and you are serving it. When confronted with such a bald alternative the choice has to be made, because as everyone knows you cannot serve two masters at the same time.

It would be true to say that the options open to us

are either that we serve God, in which case our money will serve Him and us, or we serve money, in which case we will probably expect God to serve us in various ways including helping us make more money!

Use Worldly Wealth to Make Friends

Having encouraged His disciples to be more shrewd in their dealings with life in general, and money in particular, and having reminded them that they must be astute enough to recognize that if God is not their God, money probably will be their god, He added one more startling instruction. "I tell you, use worldly wealth to gain friends for yourselves, so that when it is gone, you will be welcomed into eternal dwellings."

On the surface it would appear that the Master was encouraging His disciples to use their financial resources to ensure their eternal salvation! Countless believers would be askance at such a thought! It sounds almost as if He was encouraging such practices as the sale of indulgences, a thought that would make Martin Luther and John Calvin turn in their graves!

Taken out of its context, this verse could easily be seen to flatly contradict Peter's strong statement, "For you know that it was not with perishable things such as silver or gold that you were redeemed" (1 Pet. 1:18). To understand the Lord's instruction at this point we must remember the prevailing situation at the time He was speaking. People were encouraged in those days to express their love for the Lord in a number of ways, but particular emphasis was placed on "prayer, fasting and giving alms." When Christ moved among the people of His day He recognized that in many cases their prayers were performances, their fasting was farcical, and their alms-giving was attention-getting. He roundly condemned these things but was careful to stress that He expected His disciples to continue the practices as originally devised while carefully avoiding the abuses that were so common. Accordingly, He had already taught His disciples that they would be expected to demonstrate their devotion to the Father and His Son through their giving (among other things). This would no more earn their salvation than would praying or fasting, but it would, if done from a genuine heart, be an evidence that they had tasted of the Lord's goodness and grace.

In addition to giving being an evidence of grace received, however, the Lord in this parable reminds His followers that giving can be a means of influencing people for the Kingdom. In fact, this correct use of money could be so effective that it would lead people to an experience of the Kingdom! Jesus firmly believed that money given, as unto the Lord in gratitude but unto the needy in compassion, would touch many a heart and lead the recipients to repentance and faith and thus to the "eternal dwellings." He then sketches the exciting scene of those who have given in such a way that people are blessed through their benevolence, being welcomed in eternity by those who were there ahead of them because of their giving. Imagine the excitement for all concerned to meet the person whose benevolence was a means of leading you to glory, and on the other side of the coin being privileged to meet the people in glory because the Lord's goodness and grace stimulated you to give!

Affluence and Influence

Translated into modern terms this parable has a message of extreme force. The affluent nations of the world have a great number of disciples of Christ living happily in the blessings of affluence but not always with a sense of the blessings that affluence can provide for the underprivileged. For instance, the church of Christ in the underdeveloped nations of the world is short of trained leadership. A brilliant Indian minister, with a doctorate in theology from Oxford, told me recently that he had the materials and the methodology to train hundreds of men and women for the ministry in India but not the finances to support the translators, teachers, and staff necessary to get the job done. When I asked what kind of financial help he needed he quoted figures that showed that he could support a team of people for three years to get the scheme off the ground for the same amount of money it would take to keep one missionary in India for one year in language school.

In the same area of India I spoke to another Christian leader who showed how he could develop a market gardening project to bring work to the unemployed, produce food for the undernourished and establish a financial base for the evangelization of the whole area where only paganism was known, for the price of one luxury automobile!

Illustrations of this nature could be multiplied ad infinitum. But these two will suffice to show how, if Western believers would use their mammon shrewdly, they would not only be able to show their love for the Lord, who gave Himself, by their giving, but they would be able to use their mammon to help others find the Saviour. And they could anticipate getting to heaven and being met by some bright shining faces saying, "Welcome to eternal dwellings and thanks for helping us get here too!"

12 Richness— A Matter of Evaluation
Luke 16:14-31—The Rich Man and Lazarus

The Pharisees, who loved money, heard all this and were sneering at Jesus. He said to them, "You are the ones who justify yourselves in the eyes of men, but God knows your hearts. What is highly valued among men is detestable in God's sight.

"The Law and the Prophets were proclaimed until John. Since that time, the good news of the kingdom of God is being preached, and everyone is forcing his way into it. It is easier for heaven and earth to disappear than for the least stroke of a pen to drop out of the Law.

"Anyone who divorces his wife and marries another woman commits adultery, and the man who marries a divorced woman commits adultery.

"There was a rich man who was dressed in purple

and fine linen and lived in luxury every day. At his gate was laid a beggar named Lazarus, covered with sores and longing to eat what fell from the rich man's table. Even the dogs came and licked his sores.

"The time came when the beggar died and the angels carried him to Abraham's side. The rich man also died and was buried. In hell, where he was in torment, he looked up and saw Abraham far away, with Lazarus by his side. So he called to him, 'Father Abraham, have pity on me and send Lazarus to dip the tip of his finger in water and cool my tongue, because I am in agony in this fire.'

"But Abraham replied, 'Son, remember that in your lifetime you received your good things, while Lazarus received bad things, but now he is comforted here and you are in agony. And besides all this, between us and you a great chasm has been fixed, so that those who want to go from here to you cannot, nor can anyone cross over from there to us.'

"He answered, 'Then I beg you, father, send Lazarus to my father's house, for I have five brothers. Let him warn them, so that they will not also come to this place of torment.'

"Abraham replied, 'They have Moses and the Prophets; let them listen to them.'

"'No, father Abraham,' he said, 'but if someone from the dead goes to them, they will repent.'

"He said to him, 'If they do not listen to Moses and the Prophets, they will not be convinced even if someone rises from the dead.'"

Some years ago when I was traveling in South America I was taken by a missionary into the jungles of Peru. We flew in a light aircraft through low cloud and sheeting rain until we sighted a tiny cluster of huts on a river bank. Because there was a possibility of logs or other solid materials being in the water we flew along the river straining our eyes to see if it was safe to put the floatplane down. All appeared to be well so we held our breath and made a safe landing and taxied up to the steep bank on which the huts stood.

One of the Indians clad in a skimpy loincloth and an expansive smile came out to meet us. He carried a bow about six feet long, which was about one foot longer than himself. While my missionary friend carried on a conversation I indicated that I would like to hold the bow and the Indian obliged. As I was holding it I thought I might as well show how strong I was so I proceeded to stretch the bow, and that was my first mistake! It was too powerful for me! The Indian looked in amazement and then burst into howls of laughter. The sight of such a big man as myself with a pale face and big nose, wearing all sorts of odd clothes and flying around in a plane, but unable to stretch a bow, was too funny. I thought his laughter would never end. But fortunately it did because as things turned out he needed to catch his breath in time for the next bout of laughter.

As we turned to leave the villagers who had gathered round us, my feet slipped in the thick mud. I landed on my back and started to slide with my feet in the air in the direction of the muddy waters of the river in which all manner of unspeakable monsters lived. Furiously I tried to stop my downward progress, but the more I struggled the more momentum I gained until caked and soaked, I finally came to rest in the water. The jungles rocked with laughter. Monkeys, startled by such a display of frivolity headed, chattering, for the topmost branches while I, caked in mud from head to toe, climbed into the plane muttering to the pilot, "Let's get out of here."

As we circled the village the Indians were still standing on the bank waving and convulsed with laughter!

What's So Funny?

For a long time I had wondered about humor. But after that particular experience I realized that even people who have just arrived out of the bronze age have a sense of humor not unlike ours. Of course, there are many things that make people laugh, but the downfall of someone else makes for laughter around the world! There is an element of malicious glee about that kind of laughter, particularly if the person who falls conveys an aura of superiority and those who laugh were feeling inferior, or uncomfortable.

Jesus was subjected to this kind of response after He gave His talk about money. He had given the runaround, to the Pharisees and they were feeling decidedly sore about it. But they didn't give up, and relentlessly they went after Him in an effort to trip Him up. When He said, "You cannot serve both God and Money" they thought He had made the mistake they were waiting for and they howled with delight.

They believed that they had money because God blessed them. In fact, their money was, to them, evidence of God's blessing on their lives and the relative poverty of Jesus was evidence of the lack of God's blessing. This was one of the few areas in which they could feel superior to Him. They were no match for Him with words. His actions left them trailing in His dust, and the popularity which He enjoyed was a bitter pill for them to swallow. But they did have money and He didn't so God must be on their side. For Him, therefore, to suggest that money could get in God's way when they knew that money was God's method of blessing was to show His ignorance of God and to demonstrate that deep down He was conscious

151

of His lowly position and was endeavoring to cover it up. So they howled with derision! At last they felt secure in their superiority!

Never one to duck an issue, the Lord came right back at them. "You are the ones who justify yourselves in the eyes of men," He said. "You have your own value systems and concentrate on the things 'highly valued among men.'" Like the rich man of the parable they "lived in luxury every day."

Every society has its way of establishing the worth of an individual and then has a clear system of demonstrating this worth in measurable and recognizable symbols. For instance, when I was a businessman in England traveling to the financial centers of the big cities I could easily recognize the status symbols of the businessmen. Brief cases, rolled umbrellas, stiff white collars, grey ties, and bowler hat carefully brushed in a certain way and, of course, the dark conservative suit.

Since moving to America I have learned to read the signals of worth of the black community and the white, suburban community, the society of the deep South, and that of the youthful generation. But like the society of the Pharisees, these signals and symbols of worth may be crossed signals and misleading symbols. Jesus added, "You are the ones who justify yourselves in the eyes of men but God knows your hearts. What is highly valued among men is detestable in God's sight." This should not be regarded as a blanket condemnation of all that man may regard as important. Because, obviously, man has been known to be right about some things. But the point the Master was making was that all that they regarded as being worthy about mankind was not necessarily so. And all that they projected as symbols of worthy status could be more accurately recognized as symbols of something quite different. To press home this unpalatable truth the Master told a parable that is probably His toughest.

The Rich Man and Lazarus

Pulling no punches, He told them of the rich man who lived in luxury every day who seemed oblivious to the condition of the people around him—one of whom actually begged regularly on his doorstep asking for nothing more than to be allowed to eat the scraps from the table. Lazarus, the beggar, eventually died and "the angels carried him to Abraham's side." Shortly afterwards, the rich man died too, was buried, and arrived to his intense surprise and chagrin in Hades. The rich man, who was having a terrible time, was also conscious that the former beggar was having a superb time, and that, of course, only added to his misery. The rich man asked Abraham to send the former beggar to assist him, presumably showing that he still felt some degree of superiority to Lazarus despite all the evidence to the contrary. But Abraham declined and reminded him of his own total disregard for the well-being of Lazarus while they were both on earth. Furthermore, he pointed out to the rich man that there was no way of getting from Lazarus to him. The rich man then said, "Send Lazarus to my father's house, for I have five brothers. Let him warn them." Still seeing Lazarus as someone to be sent on errands, the rich man had still not got the message. Abraham declined once more, pointing out to the rich man that his brothers had every opportunity of preparing for eternity and even if Lazarus went to them from the dead they would "not be convinced."

The Master said many unpopular things in His days on earth, but it is doubtful if He ever said anything more likely to raise the ire of His arch-opponents, the Pharisees, than what He explained in this parable. It was as if someone were to go to the most successful businessman in town and say to him, "You have your big house; your kids are in private schools; your place at the lake is beautifully equipped; your Cadillac, Porsche, Rolls and custom-made recreational vehicle are standing at the door; the new Lear jet will be delivered next week; your seats on the 50-yard line are confirmed for the next five seasons; your invitation to the White House reception has been accepted; the church board has elected you chairman; the governor wants you on a select committee; and your investment counselor just called with news of some exciting new developments and God says, "You're a big phony."

Conflict in Evaluation

For there to be such a conflict in the evaluating of lives there had to be a conflict in standards of measurement. This was exactly the point Christ was making and it has to be one of the most important topics He ever broached.

He pointed out to the Pharisees their disregard for the law particularly in their attitude to marriage and divorce. They had become so flippant in their attitudes that some of their great teachers were saying that if the wife didn't cook the dinner properly that was grounds for divorce and another had made the ruling that if a man found someone prettier than his wife he could divorce and remarry. They hadn't invented the word "incompatibility" but they were certainly familiar with the concept! Christ's concern was that they should regard themselves as such worthy people when they were living in such disregard of the divine requirements.

Then, of course, His clear denunciation of their

attitudes to the plight of the poor could not possibly be avoided. The Old Testament clearly taught the principle of responsibility to unfortunate people and this the Pharisees carefully avoided and ignored, all the time claiming to be such worthy people.

In the parable the Master clearly indicated that His listeners were like the brothers of the rich man who would not prepare for eternity even if someone returned from the dead. This condemnation was all the more striking and powerful because it was directed to those who regarded themselves as the protectors of truth and the guardians of orthodoxy. Whatever their personal evaluation, however, the Master was totally convinced that their standards of evaluation were inaccurate and, therefore, their conclusions about their own worthiness were completely erroneous.

Evaluating Genuine Worth

As we all know it is relatively simple to point out what people are doing wrong but it is not always as easy to show them what is necessary for them to do things correctly. Critics are more easily produced than performers, as attendance at any professional sporting event will readily demonstrate! The Master did not fit in the category of "critic-period" I'm glad to say. He showed how to evaluate genuine worth after He grabbed the attention of those who were making some terrible mistakes on the subject. "God knows the hearts" summarizes what He had to say on this. There is a major difference between external values, which are measured by external symbols, and internal values, which can be measured only by the standards of the God who knows our hearts.

Every person who is remotely in touch with reality knows that on some occasions he has been praised for something that society regarded as being most praise-worthy, but which, in fact, was far from praise-worthy. Like the man who gives to charity not from a charitable nature, but from a calculating attitude. He knows that the publicity will be most valuable and the tax write-off is what his accountant advised!

To balance things out a little we have probably seen things go the other way too! Feeling very benevolent and gracious we have done something particularly worthwhile at considerable expenditure of time and energy only to have someone attribute bad motives to us. We have been most hurt by the injustice of their attitude and the lack of appreciation of our real worth. But at the root of the problem is the fact that things aren't always what they appear to be!

Having recognized this and opened ourselves to the main evaluating factor—the judgment of God on what our hearts are really saying behind the things that our bodies are doing—we can begin to explore some exciting possibilities.

Law of Love

Jesus said that God had given His law to people and that this law was summarized in two concepts: Love for God and love for people. This law was taught regularly to the people of Israel and at special times God sent His prophets to underline the message of the law and remind the people of the practical things that they must do to work it out. One after the other, the prophets came and went (often in very uncomfortable ways!). But to a large extent the people of Israel rejected what they had to say. Eventually John the Baptist arrived on the scene and reminded the people that God had promised to be their God and bring them into the blessing of His plan and that they should live lovingly and joyfully in obedience to Him. Many recognized their sin and shortcomings. They admitted that they had not conducted themselves in a manner worthy of those who had special relationships with God and they repented and were baptized by John as a public testimony to their repentance and an open declaration of their intent to live obediently before the Lord as an expression of appreciation for His grace.

These people were ripe for the message Jesus then brought to them. A message that those who come to repentance and faith will enjoy the benefits of the Kingdom of God not only in heaven eventually, but on earth immediately. The people of the Kingdom will be those whose hearts have been shattered by their phoniness, and warmed by the forgiving power of God through His Son. Their lives will show the difference that has been worked by the message of the Kingdom. Instead of the cold heart of indifference to the principles of God and the extremities of mankind, there is a warmth of concern that the things of God be primary, the principles of God be adhered to, and the people God made be treated graciously and lovingly in the name of the Lord.

Jesus said that, since John preached and He had amplified what God was offering in the Kingdom, many people were "forcing [their] way into it." There had been great response, but not among the people to whom He was talking at the moment. They didn't want to know about love, they wanted to be free to love only themselves. They didn't want to know about sin, they wanted only to talk about their own self-righteousness. For them repentance and faith were unnecessary words. The contrast between the wealthy, selfish, self-righteous people who laughed at Christ's reminder of the dangers of wealth becoming a god and the administering of that wealth becoming a passion, and the humble people, who like the beggar had an open heart to the Lord, was striking in the extreme.

It goes without saying that if people's actions can be misleading it is also extremely difficult to read a person's heart. This being the case, we should be very careful before determining our own worthiness in any given situation and, of course, we should exercise great care and compassion in endeavoring to evaluate the worthiness of another person at any given time. This degree of difficulty has led many people to desist from any attempts at evaluation, but this is purely an evasion of a difficult but necessary task.

We should seek to evaluate our lives and those whom we love and serve in order that we might encourage each other and build each other up. But, bearing in mind the ease with which we can be wrong, we need great humility and much compassion and understanding.

Final Reckoning of Worth

There is one further consideration that should always be borne in mind. Granted the difficulties of establishing worth in today's world by God's standards, it is encouraging to know that there will be a final reckoning by God of that which is truly worthy. The standards of evaluation will be the response, or lack of it, to the prophetic message of God's unchanging law and the glorious development of that message through the intervention of the Christ in establishing His Kingdom in the hearts of men and women.

The worthy in the final reckoning are not the rich or the poor, the elite or the underprivileged. The worthy are those whose hard hearts have been broken by the love of God. Their perverse hearts have been captured by the forgiving grace of God and they have, from a glad heart, served Him and finally gone to their eternal reward. There are rich people with humbled, forgiven hearts and they will be in glory alongside forgiven, poor, underprivileged people. There will also be lost rich people and banished poor people. We should no more deify the poor than we should vilify the rich. To do either is to use standards of measurement foreign to the Kingdom. We should recognize that it is the heart that counts and the attitude of the heart to the Lord.

We have no record that those who laughed at the beginning of the parable stopped laughing and wept for their lost condition at the end. If the response was normal, probably some did and some didn't. To realize this impresses upon us the immensity of the load carried by those who know that God knows hearts. So far is this removed from the thinking of the man in the street, as well as the man in the gutter, that monumental effort is needed by those who know to inform those who are ignorant, either by careful design or careless indifference.

Even the rich man turned evangelist when he realized the lostness of the lost! But his approach to evangelism was as confused as his approach to life. No one can gainsay his newfound compassion but we must gainsay his understanding of the human heart. His brothers would no more turn from their sinful life-styles and be reconciled to God than the rich man would before his departure. His thinking that the sight of a resurrected body would do the trick was an evidence of his lack of understanding of the ways of God in the hearts of men. Certainly if they had seen someone return from the dead they would have been startled, perhaps even to the point of being so frightened that they might even promise to love God if He would take the apparition away and stop scaring them! But it takes more than a good scare to change a person's heart. It takes honest scrutiny of God's Word and steadfast response to Him.

They say life is full of surprises, but death will be much fuller! Can you imagine the shock of the rich man when he arrived in Hades? Can you imagine his double shock when he saw the beggar in glory? Have you ever thought of the prominent luminaries who will be lost and the humble regenerate unknowns who will be in glory? Doesn't it make you want to be "heart ready" and lead others to the same preparedness?